Praise for *Artisan Bread in Five Minutes a Day* and *The New Artisan Bread in Five Minutes a Day*

"If man cannot live by bread alone, it may be because Jeff Hertzberg and Zoë François didn't publish their book sooner.... [They've] developed a method that makes any home into a mini artisan bake shop.... Hertzberg and François' practical, common-sense method…is, quite simply, genius." —*Chicago Tribune*

"Every step of Zoë and Jeff's adventures in bread has been fascinating and delicious for us, the home bread bakers who follow them, but this book might be their most exciting yet because they've incorporated years of readers' questions, problems, and discoveries into every chapter. This is truly the all-you've-ever-wanted-to-know edition. And there are plenty of photographs . . . at last!" —**Dorie Greenspan, James Beard Award–winning author of** *Around My French Table* **and owner of Beurre & Sel cookies**

"If holiday gift-givers are aiming to buy one new cookbook title for the bakers in their lives, they should look no further." —*Minneapolis Star Tribune*

"A fun, easy-to-follow collection for those who aren't afraid to shun baking traditions." —*Publishers Weekly*

"With this revised edition, Herzberg and François continue to perfect their already easy and immensely popular bread-baking method. Essential." —*Library Journal*

Praise for *Healthy Bread in Five Minutes a Day*

"Zoë François and Jeff Hertzberg have amazingly demystified the arcane and delightful world of artisan bread. Now, on the heels of time sensitivity (Hello… 5 minutes??? Really? Yes!), comes a baking book for the health-conscious, and it couldn't be more timely. Bottom line, I would crawl across a desert of broken glass to hop into their loaf pan. . . ." —**Andrew Zimmern, Travel Channel host, food writer, and radio personality**

"It's a vast improvement over the laborious process of making artisan breads using classic methods. . . in their new book, Hertzberg and François have gone one step further… baking breads that use less sugar, healthy grains, fruits and vegetables, and are friendly to those with allergies or food sensitivities. . ." —**The Associated Press**

"We tried some of the recipes; we love 'em. … Honestly, this is the nicest, softest whole wheat sandwich bread I've ever made." —**P. J. Hamel,** *KingArthurFlour.com*

"This is the much-anticipated sequel to the wildly popular *Artisan Bread in Five Minutes a Day*… you'll be able to use the no-knead storage dough method with even healthier recipes. . . fabulous cookbooks… yummy but easy recipes!" —*Mother Earth News*

"*Healthy Bread in Five Minutes a Day*… is a cookbook that just might change your life. . . Brilliant? I say yes! I sometimes read cookbooks like novels, and this book… is filled with good ideas about healthy bread baking. . ." —*Glamour.com*

Praise for *Gluten-Free Artisan Bread in Five Minutes a Day*

"Quick artisan breads, no kneading, no proofing, no punching down. . . You'll be on your way to delicious bread in no time." — **Living Free's** *Gluten Free & More* **magazine**

"For gluten-free bread that tastes like it came from a European bakery, it's worth the wait."—*The Oregonian*

"I baked a flatbread for a gluten-free friend—and no one suspected it was not its floury cousin. . . the book's recipes for blending your own gluten-free flours are easy and fail-safe." —*Minneapolis Star Tribune*

"Hertzberg and François offer foolproof recipes for [gluten-free] bread. . ." —*The Columbus Dispatch*

"The recipes make you wonder why you use wheat when such fabulous bread can be made without it. . . . We can personally vouch for the doughnuts. OMG."—**Minneapolis-St. Paul** *City Pages*

Praise for *Artisan Pizza and Flatbread in Five Minutes a Day*

"A wealth of information on how to prepare this world-famous dish in minutes… an outstanding book for working parents that are interested in serving healthier meals to their families during the week."—*Seattle Post-Intelligencer*

"Will get the baker on your list jumping with glee. Thin crust, thick crust, dipping breads and desserts— think good old pizza margherita, Turkish pita boats, and banana cream hand pies—all in the time it takes to heat up the oven." —**The Associated Press**

"You want this book… endless variations in pizza crusts, sauces, and toppings, plus troubleshooting tips and instructions on tossing pies pizza parlor-style right in your own kitchen." —*Mother Earth News*

"It sounds too good to be true, but [*Artisan Pizza and Flatbread in Five Minutes a Day*]… has a technique to prep the dough that will make you wonder why you've been buying pizza dough."—*McClatchy-Tribune*

"[Their first book]. . . banished the fear of kneading for a whole generation of cooks. Now, with their newest adventure. . . the duo takes on an even bigger task: that completely personal and often polariz-ing topic—crust. . . with a truckload of recipes that are exciting and intriguing to even the casual pizza maker. Basically, it's a reason to broaden your pizza boundaries and become the pizzaioli *you've always dreamed of being.*" —*Mpls.St.Paul Magazine*

"It doesn't get any easier than this… thin-crust pizza? … Jeff and Zoë to the rescue, again! . . . no spe-cial skills needed, no fancy ingredients, no hard-to-find ingredients… Sicilian style? Awesome—chewy, crunchy crust, full of big holes, and perfectly cooked toppings." —**P. J. Hamel,** *KingArthurFlour.com*

Holiday and Celebration
BREAD
in Five Minutes a Day

ALSO BY ZOË FRANÇOIS AND JEFF HERTZBERG, M.D.

The New Artisan Bread in Five Minutes a Day:
Revised and Updated with New Recipes

The New Healthy Bread in Five Minutes a Day:
Revised and Updated with New Recipes

Artisan Bread in Five Minutes a Day:
The Discovery that Revolutionizes Home Baking

Healthy Bread in Five Minutes a Day:
100 New Recipes Featuring Whole Grains, Fruits
Vegetables, and Gluten-Free Ingredients

Artisan Pizza and Flatbread in Five Minutes a Day:
The Homemade Bread Revolution Continues

Gluten-Free Artisan Bread in Five Minutes a Day:
The Baking Revolution Continues with 90 New, Delicious, and
Easy Recipes Made with Gluten-Free Flours

Holiday and Celebration
BREAD
in Five Minutes a Day

SWEET AND DECADENT BAKING
FOR EVERY OCCASION

Zoë François and Jeff Hertzberg, M.D.

Photographs by Sarah Kieffer and Zoë François

St. Martin's Press ❧ New York

www.stmartins.com

Designed by Philip Mazzone

Photographs copyright © 2018 by Sarah Kieffer and Zoë François

The Library of Congress Cataloging-in-Publication Data is available upon request.

ISBN 978-1-250-07756-1 (hardcover)
ISBN 978-1-4668-8977-4 (ebook)

Our books may be purchased in bulk for promotional, educational, or business use. Please contact your local bookseller or the Macmillan Corporate and Premium Sales Department at 1-800-221-7945, extension 5442, or by email at MacmillanSpecialMarkets@macmillan.com.

First Edition: November 2018

10 9 8 7 6 5 4 3 2 1

To Sally, who shaped my view of the world through her love of art and great food

—Z.F.

To Laura, Rachel, and Julia, the holiday bakers at my house

—J.H.

CONTENTS

CONTENTS

ACKNOWLEDGMENTS

Cookbook deals for unknown authors without TV shows were a long shot when we started this adventure in 2007—and they still are. On top of that, we knew bread baking, but we didn't know publishing. So we needed some luck, and some generous people to help us. Our most heartfelt thanks go to our first editor at Thomas Dunne Books, the late Ruth Cavin. She liked our idea and decided to publish us. Decisive is good. Otherwise this would still be just an eccentric family project. Ruth passed our baby to Pete Wolverton, who has been our trusted editor for six more books, plus the rest of the St. Martin's Press team: Jennifer Donovan, John Karle, Justine Sha, Cathy Turiano, Elizabeth Curione, Michael Storrings, Nikolaas Eickelbeck, Jonathan Bennett, Brant Janeway, Jordan Hanley, and Judy Hunt (who created another great index). Since a book is only as good as its editors, we'd like to give a special thanks to Cheryl Redmond, for her extraordinarily thoughtful reading of the book. Lynne Rossetto Kasper, Sally Swift, Jennifer Luebke, and Jen Russell of *The Splendid Table* radio program gave us our first (and subsequent) national exposure on National Public Radio when they took Jeff's call on Lynne's radio show, which gave us the opportunity to meet Ruth in the first place. Lynne also gave great advice and connected us with our top-notch literary agent, Jane Dystel, who has, with Miriam Goderich and Lauren Abramo, steadily and lovingly guided us through this wild ride for twelve years, seven books, and five translations.

We've also had great friends, family, and readers to act as recipe testers. They baked endlessly and offered us their honest criticism and praise. Once they started using our recipes, we understood that this would be a book for everyone—avid bakers and non-bakers alike. That was a revelation. So we owe our book to all of you, too numerous to mention by name, but if you've bought our books, visited our website, followed us on Facebook, or found us on Pinterest or Instagram, we're so very grateful. It really takes a village to raise a book. There are several folks who helped with Herculean strength and monumental inspiration to make this book come alive: Jen Sommerness; Craig and Patricia Neal; Lorraine Neal; Leslie Bazzett; Jay, Tracey, Gavin, and Megan Berkowitz; the late Sarah Berkowitz; the late Barbara Neal; Marion and John Callahan; Barb Davis; Fran Davis; Anna and Ewart François; Kathy Kasnoff and Lyonel Norris; Andy Small; Andrew Hachiya; Troy Meyers; Kristin Neal and Bill Friedman; Carey, Heather, and Victoria Neal; Sally Simmons and David van de Sande; and Amy Vang.

From the publishing world, writers Beth Fouhy and Peggy Orenstein helped us navigate the murky waters of book publicity. The great team at Craftsy.com produced Zoë's fabulous instructional video, "Artisan Bread in Minutes."

Gratitude to colleagues in our baking and culinary adventures past and present: Robin Asbell; Steven Brown of Tilia and St. Genevieve; Adam Cohn of Adam Cohn Law; Abby Dodge; Stephen Durfee of the Culinary Institute of America; Barbara Fenzl of Les Gourmettes Cooking School; Michelle Gayer of The Salty Tart; Dorie Greenspan; Thomas Gumpel; P. J. Hamel and Jeffrey Hamelman of King Arthur Flour; Bill Hanes, Kelly Olson, and Linda Nelson of Red Star Yeast; Kim Harbinson; Molly Herrmann of Kitchen in the Market; Ragavan Iyer (who sat down with Zoë in 2005 and explained how the publishing world *really* works); Dusti Kugler, Kelly Lainsbury, and Madeline Hill of Food Works; Brenda Langton of Spoonriver restaurant and the Minneapolis Bread Festival; Kevin Masse of The FeedFeed; Tracy Morgan; Silvana Nardone; Stephanie Meyer of FreshTart.com; Riad Nasr, Karl Benson, and Marie Dwyer at Cooks of Crocus Hill; Peter Reinhart; the entire team at Quang; Suvir Saran and

Charlie Burd of American Masala; Eliza Woolston Sheffield and Ann Moth of Blue Star Cooking; Tara Steffen of Emile Henry; Jamie Schler; Maria Speck; Joy Summers; and Andrew Zimmern.

And thank you to Jeff Lin of BustOutSolutions.com, for maintaining our website. Graham (Zoë's husband) gave immeasurable moral support and designed and created our website, BreadIn5.com, and Laura Silver (Jeff's wife) made sure that Thomas Dunne Books got manuscripts that were already vetted by an experienced editor.

Sarah Kieffer has always made us look great by creating content for the website, and led us through the crazy world of social media and styling for our books. Now she's taken our book to the next level of beauty with her genius photography. She is pure talent and brings the joy to work.

Rachel Hertzberg, Jeff's daughter, did research and lent her beautiful writing to the various holiday bread headnotes. There are so many cultures and traditions, and we trusted her to help us do them justice.

Most of all we are thankful for the love and support of our families: Zoë's husband, Graham, and her two boys, Henri and Charlie; and Jeff's wife, Laura, and his girls, Rachel and Julia. They're our best taste testers and most honest critics.

THE SECRET

Mix Enough Dough for Several Loaves and Store It in the Refrigerator

It is so easy to have freshly baked breads and yeasted pastry when you want them, even during the holidays, with only minutes of active effort for each loaf. First, mix the ingredients from any of our recipes into a container all at once, then let them sit to rise. Now you are ready to shape and bake the bread, or you can refrigerate the dough and use it over the next several days—or even weeks, if you freeze it! Each recipe makes enough dough for multiple loaves. When you want fresh-baked bread, take a piece of the dough from the container and shape it into a loaf. Let it rest and then bake. Your house will smell like a celebration, and your family and friends will love you for it.

PREFACE

This is the book I've been waiting ten years to write. I've always managed to persuade Jeff to dedicate a substantial chapter in each of our books to the pastry side of bread, but in this book we get to focus exclusively on these beautiful, beloved recipes. I love all holidays and the foods we eat to celebrate them, but it's the sweets that truly move me. Growing up, I had a grandmother who baked a dozen types of cookies at Christmas and another who served the largest, fluffiest challah during Rosh Hashanah. I was gifted with many holidays to celebrate, each one with a rich tradition of foods. Later in life, my husband's family introduced me to a whole new world of flavors from Trinidad (which is a true melting pot of cuisines). I have traveled the world in search of food, pastry, and bread, and now I get to share that love on these pages. —Zoë

The best thing about holidays, or really any celebration, is gathering with family and community to share time and great food together. Every culture in the world has its traditional, festive holiday recipes, and we set out to find them. Some were shared by our readers—one asked how to adapt her grandmother's Christmas stollen—or from people we met in the most unlikely places, like the airport limo driver in Denver who told us about Moroccan *meloui.* There is so much love and joy connected to these breads and the memories they evoke.

This is a book devoted to the sweeter side of bread—sweet-tasting, of course, but sweet for the soul, too. We've always struck a balance in our books between our love of carbs and sweets and our desire to maintain a healthy lifestyle. We are, after all, a pastry chef and a physician, writing books about bread, so there's bound to be a push and pull. Creating a book about holiday breads that are mostly full of sugar and butter can pose a philosophical dilemma. Even Zoë, a pastry chef by training, is as conscientious about what she eats and as careful to bake healthfully for her family as Jeff, who's a physician. And what we've discovered in our twelve-year collaboration comes down to this: moderation. Enjoy life, enjoy bread, enjoy sweets; just do it all in moderation, and even the most decadent treats can be part of a healthy lifestyle. We've included recipes that are made with whole grains and alternative sweeteners, but we don't use artificial sweeteners or synthetic fats, since we don't love the way they taste. If you have specific dietary needs, you may want to consider our book ***The New Healthy Bread in Five Minutes a Day***, which uses whole grains and focuses on a healthy list of ingredients, or for non-wheat eaters, our ***Gluten-Free Artisan Bread in Five Minutes a Day***. These books include delicious, indulgent holiday breads too. Most importantly, enjoy all the bread you bake!

How did a doctor and a pastry chef set out to write seven bread books together? This astonishing, crazy adventure—one that started as nothing more than a little project between friends, but has become **the best-selling bread cookbook series of all time**—began in our kids' music class in 2003. It was an unlikely place for co-authors to meet, but in the swirl of toddlers, musical chairs, and xylophones, there was time for the grownups to talk. Zoë said that she was a pastry chef and baker who'd been trained at the Culinary Institute of America (CIA). What a fortuitous coincidence. Jeff wasn't a food professional at all, but he'd been tinkering for years with an easy, fast method for making homemade bread. He begged her to try a secret recipe he'd been developing. The secret? Mix a big batch of dough and store it in the refrigerator. It was promising, but it needed work.

Zoë was skeptical. Jeff had been trained as a scientist, not as a chef. On the other hand, that might be an advantage when it came to experimenting with new approaches to homemade bread. So we did a taste test—and luckily, Zoë loved the results. Better yet, she was willing to develop a book with an amateur. Our approach produces fantastic homemade loaves without the enormous time investment required by the traditional artisanal method.

This had been an opportunity that was just waiting for the right moment. In 2000, Jeff had called in to Lynne Rossetto Kasper's National Public Radio show, *The Splendid Table*, to get advice on getting a cookbook idea into print. Lynne was supportive and helpful on the air, but more importantly, a St. Martin's Press editor named Ruth Cavin, who'd been listening to Lynne's show, phoned *The Splendid Table* and asked for a book proposal. The rest, as they say, is history, as ***Artisan Bread in Five Minutes a Day*** was published in 2007.

We were first-time authors, with a great idea but no track record. Worse, we were far from being celebrity chefs, which was fast becoming a requirement for cookbook success. But we knew if people got their hands on this method, they would use it. The only problem was proving that to the publisher. St. Martin's gave us a small budget for photographs, which meant only eight color pictures, plus a smattering of black-and-white how-to shots. We'd have loved to have had more, but were thrilled to have any. We may have the lack of photos to thank for the birth of our website.

We knew that people would need guidance to bake bread, and having lots of pictures would help more than just about anything. We hoped that we had a winner: the book *plus* our new website (BreadIn5.com), chock-full of pictures and with its two authors eager to answer reader questions themselves. Our website exceeded our wildest hopes—it became the center of a five-minute-a-day bread-baking community, with nearly a quarter-million pageviews per month. We're on duty every day—to answer questions, respond to comments, and post about what we're baking and working on. It's become part of our daily lives and our creative process. Through the questions and comments from readers, we've learned what works, what could have been easier, and what new breads people want. So our follow-up books, ***Healthy Bread in Five Minutes a Day*** (2009), ***Artisan Pizza and Flatbread in Five Minutes a Day*** (2011), ***Gluten-Free Artisan Bread in Five Minutes a Day*** (2014), and new editions of the first two are based on requests that came from our readers, who reached us through our website, our Facebook page (Facebook.com/Breadin5), our Twitter identity (@ArtisanBreadIn5), Pinterest (Breadin5), and Instagram (@breadin5). We've met thousands of bakers just like us—busy people who love fresh bread but don't necessarily have all day to make it. It's been a joy.

Everyone loves great bread, and here is a way to make it that's fast, super easy, and *cheap* (under seventy-five cents a loaf). After six books and 750,000 copies sold, we're so happy to be back with this holiday book. It's really a community effort with the help of our readers, from whom we've learned so much. Thanks to you, we discovered what works well, what's complicated, and what needs more explanation. In this new book, we want to share everything we've learned during this ten-year conversation.

First off, people asked for more holiday recipes! We've included breads from all over the globe and many different holidays, including Christmas breads from Europe, Middle Eastern Ramadan pita, traditional Easter breads, challah for Jewish celebrations, Indian breads, and many more. We also included breads that can be served on any given day to create a celebration, like monkey bread, cinnamon rolls, coffee cake, and everyone's favorites, doughnuts and croissants.

These holiday breads are often as beautiful as they are delicious, so we wanted more pictures to inspire you to create the recipes, so for the first time we've included pictures for each bread. Our breads come to life in more than 100 how-to photos and finished breads. We're thrilled with our new photos, and we hope they'll inspire you to bake every day.

These recipes are as easy as the ones in all of our books, but some require you to handle the dough slightly differently than we've had you do in the past, so Tips and Techniques (Chapter 4) and Ingredients (Chapter 2) are bigger and better than ever before.

We've incorporated some of our readers' frequently asked questions that kept popping up on the website. All of the dough recipes are written with weight equivalents in addition to cup-measures for flour and other ingredients. The new electronic scales have really simplified weighing for folks who want to do it. It's a timesaver, yields more consistent results, and there is no need to wash the measuring cups. And the dough recipes are set up so readers can customize the salt to their own palates.

Our goal in all of our ***Bread in Five Minutes a Day*** books has been to help home bakers make great daily breads and sweets but still have a life outside the kitchen. To all of you who helped us make this series happen, thank you. Together we've started a revolution—opening up hundreds of thousands of homes to the satisfaction and delights of homemade bread. And most important, we've had fun.

We want you to have fun baking, too. If you worry about the bread, it won't taste as good. Happy Holidays, or just Tuesday!

1

INTRODUCTION

The Secret to Making Bread in Five Minutes a Day: Refrigerating Pre-Mixed Homemade Dough

The handmade bread that was available all over the country many generations ago wasn't a rarefied delicacy. Everyone knew what it was and took it for granted. It was not a stylish addition to affluent lifestyles; it was a simple comfort food brought here by modest immigrants. Recipes were shared by grandmothers and grandfathers from one generation to the next. In the 1950s, that tradition was replaced by packaged breads that were quick and more convenient but lacked any flavor and the shared tradition of making bread from scratch.

Great breads, handmade by artisans, were still available, but they'd become part of the serious (and seriously expensive) food phenomenon that had swept the country. The bread bakery was no longer on every corner—now it was a destination. And nobody's grandmother would ever have paid six dollars for a loaf of bread.

So we decided to do something about it. When *Artisan Bread in Five Minutes a Day* came out in 2007, it was our attempt to help people re-create the great ethnic and American breads of years past, in their own homes, *without investing serious time in the process.* Using our straightforward, fast, and easy recipes, anyone will be able to create artisan bread and pastry at home with minimal equipment.

But who has time to make bread every day? After years of experimentation, it turns out that *we* do, and with a method as fast as ours, you can too. We solved the time problem *and* produced top-quality artisan loaves without a bread machine. We worked out the master recipes during busy years of career transition and starting families (our now-adult kids delight in the pleasures of home-baked bread). Our lightning-fast method lets us find the time to bake great bread every day. We developed this method to recapture the daily artisan-bread experience without further crunching our limited time—and it works!

Traditional breads made the old-fashioned way need a lot of attention; they must be kneaded until resilient, set to rise, punched down, and allowed to rise again. Very few busy people can go through this every day, if ever. Even if your friends are all food fanatics, when was the last time you had homemade bread at a dinner party?

So we went to work. Over the years, we figured out how to subtract the various steps that make the classic technique so time-consuming, and identified a few that couldn't be omitted. It all came down to one fortuitous discovery:

Pre-mixed, pre-risen, high-moisture dough keeps well in the refrigerator.

This is the linchpin of all our *Bread in Five Minutes a Day* books. By pre-mixing high-moisture dough (without kneading) and then storing it, we've made daily bread baking an easy activity; the only steps you do every day are shaping and baking. Other books have considered refrigerating dough, but only for a few days. Many others have omitted the kneading step. But none has tested the capacity of wet dough to be long-lived in your refrigerator. When dough is mixed with adequate liquid (this dough is wetter than most you may have worked with), it can be stored in the refrigerator for several days (or be frozen for even longer). And kneading this kind of dough adds little to the overall product; you just don't have to do it. In fact, overhandling many of our stored dough recipes can limit the volume and rise that you get with our method. Having said that, in this book, you will see the word "knead" come up, but we promise it's just for a few seconds, nothing laborious. With our egg and butter doughs, it gives the gluten more strength and encouragement to be "turned" a few times before shaping, which results in a lighter and higher loaf. Since many of these holiday breads are filled will all kinds of tasty additions, it is nice to have the extra lift and lightness. That, in a nutshell, is how you make artisan breads with only five minutes a day of active effort. In this book, there are some breads that take a few more minutes to achieve the full beauty of their traditional shapes, but they're worth it.

A one- or two-week supply of dough is made in advance and stored in the refrigerator. Measuring and mixing the dough takes less than fifteen minutes. Kneading, at least in the mixing process, as we've said, is not necessary. Every day, cut off a hunk of dough from the storage container and briefly shape it without kneading. Allow it to rest briefly on the counter, and then toss it in the oven. We don't count the rest time (twenty minutes or more depending on the recipe) or baking time (usually about thirty minutes) in our five-minute-a-day calculation, since you can be doing something else while that's happening. If you bake after dinner, the bread will stay fresh for use the next day (higher-moisture breads stay fresh longer), but the method is so convenient that you probably will find you can cut off some dough and bake a loaf every morning before your day starts (especially if you make flatbreads like pita).

Using high-moisture, pre-mixed, pre-risen dough makes most of the difficult, time-consuming, and demanding steps in traditional bread baking completely superfluous:

1. You don't need to make dough every day to have fresh bread every day: Stored dough makes wonderful fresh loaves. Only the shaping and baking steps are done daily; the rest has been done in advance.

2. It doesn't matter how you mix the dry and wet ingredients together: So long as the mixture is uniform, without any dry lumps of flour, it makes no difference whether you use a spoon, a Danish dough whisk, or a heavy-duty stand mixer. Choose based on your own convenience.

3. You don't need to "proof" yeast: Traditional recipes require that yeast be dissolved in water with a little sugar and allowed to sit for five minutes to prove that bubbles can form and the yeast is alive. But modern yeast simply doesn't fail if used before its expiration date and the baker remembers to use lukewarm, not hot, water. The high water content in our doughs further ensures that the yeast will fully hydrate and activate without a proofing step. Further storage gives it plenty of time to fully ferment the dough—our approach doesn't need the head start.

4. The dough isn't kneaded: It can be mixed and stored in the same large, lidded plastic container. No wooden board is required. There should be only one vessel to wash, plus a spoon (or a mixer). You'll never tell the difference between breads made with kneaded and unkneaded high-moisture dough, so long as you mix to a basically uniform consistency. In our method, a very quick "cloaking and shaping" step substitutes for kneading (see Chapter 5, step 4, page 50).

WHAT WE DON'T HAVE TO DO: STEPS FROM TRADITIONAL ARTISAN BAKING THAT WE OMITTED

1. Mix a new batch of dough every time we want to make bread.
2. "Proof" yeast.
3. Knead dough.
4. Rest and rise the loaves in a draft-free location—it doesn't matter!
5. Fuss over doubling or tripling of dough volume.
6. Punch down and re-rise: Never punch down stored dough!
7. Poke rising loaves to be sure they've "proofed" by leaving indentations.

Now you know why it only takes five minutes a day, not including resting and baking time.

Given these simple principles, anyone can make artisan bread at home. We'll talk about what you'll need in Chapters 2 (Ingredients) and 3 (Equipment). You don't need a professional baker's kitchen. In Chapter 4, you'll learn the tips and techniques that we've taken years to accumulate. Then, in Chapter 5, we'll lay out the basics of our method, applying them to simple white dough and several delicious variations. Chapter 5's master recipe is the model for the rest of our recipes. We suggest you read it first and bake some of its breads before trying anything else. You won't regret it. And if you want more information, we're on the Web at BreadIn5.com, where you'll find instructional text, photographs, videos, and a community of other five-minute bakers. Other easy ways to keep in touch: follow us on Instagram at @Breadin5, Twitter at @ArtisanBreadin5, on Facebook at @BreadIn5, on Pinterest at BreadIn5, or on our YouTube channel, BreadIn5.

2

INGREDIENTS

Here's a very practical guide to the ingredients we use to produce artisan loaves.

Flours and Grains

ALL-PURPOSE FLOUR: This is the staple ingredient for most of the recipes in this book. All-purpose flour is a great choice for white flour because of its medium protein content. Most of the protein in it is highly elastic gluten, which allows bread dough to trap the carbon dioxide gas produced by yeast. Without gluten, bread wouldn't rise. That's why flours that contain only minimal gluten (like rye) need to be mixed with wheat flour to make a successful loaf. Traditional bread recipes stress the need to develop gluten through kneading, which turns out *not* to be essential if you make a wet dough.

With a protein content of about 10 percent in most national brands, all-purpose flour will have adequate gluten to create a satisfying "chew" and structure in the bread.

Gluten is strengthened when the proteins align themselves into strands after water is added. This creates a network that traps gas bubbles and creates an airy interior crumb. These lined-up strands can be formed in two ways:

The dough can be kneaded: Not the way we like to spend our time. OR . . .

By using lots of water: The gluten strands become mobile enough to *align themselves.*

So creating a wet dough is the basis for all no-knead methods. It's easy to consistently achieve this moisture level with U.S. all-purpose flour. We tested our recipes with Gold Medal brand all-purpose, but most standard supermarket all-purpose products will give similar results.

We prefer unbleached flours for their natural creamy color, as well as their lack of unnecessary chemicals.

FLOUR PROTEINS: Some all-purpose flours, such as King Arthur, Dakota Maid, and most Canadian all-purpose flours, have more protein—about 11.5 percent, rather than 10 percent. They work beautifully in the recipes in this book; although the dough may be drier than with Gold Medal all-purpose flour, it doesn't make a big enough difference to matter.

Some flours have too little protein to make successful high-moisture dough—stay away from cake flour and pastry flour (around 8 percent protein). The dough just won't have the structure to form a nice loaf of bread.

BREAD FLOUR: This white flour has about 12 percent protein. For some of the breads, we wanted even more structure to hold their decorative shape, so we recommend using this "strong" flour.

WHOLE WHEAT FLOUR: Whole wheat flour contains the germ and bran of wheat, both of which are healthful and tasty. Together they add a slightly bitter, nutty flavor to bread that most people enjoy. The naturally occurring oils in wheat germ prevent formation of a crackling crust, so you're going for a different type of loaf when you start increasing the proportion of whole wheat flour. In general, you can use any kind of whole wheat flour that's available to you.

WHITE WHOLE WHEAT FLOUR: White whole wheat flour is 100 percent whole grain, but it's ground from a white wheat berry rather than the usual "red" one. It's pale-colored and mild-tasting, but it packs the same nutrition as regular whole wheat. It measures like regular whole wheat and can be used as a substitute for it. But don't expect it to taste like white flour and don't try to substitute it 1:1 for all-purpose or you'll get a dry, dense dough that won't store well at all.

STORING WHOLE WHEAT FLOUR: Oils in whole wheat flour can go rancid if stored for long periods at room temperature. So if you don't use it often, store it in an airtight container in the freezer.

RYE FLOUR: In U.S. supermarkets, choices are usually limited to the high-bran high-protein varieties, like Hodgson Mill Stone-Ground Whole Grain Rye and Bob's Red Mill Organic Stone-Ground Rye Flour. Whichever kind of rye you use, it must be paired with wheat flour, because it has little gluten and won't rise well on its own.

SEMOLINA FLOUR: Semolina is a major component of some Italian and Middle Eastern breads, where it lends a beautiful yellow color and spectacular winey-sweet flavor. The best semolina for bread is the finely ground "durum" flour. It is available from Bob's Red Mill (in groceries or online), or from mail-order sources like King Arthur Flour (see Sources, page 363). If you use flour labeled as "semolina" (commonly found in South Asian groceries), you'll find that it's usually a coarser grind and needs to be decreased in the recipes or the result can be an overly dry dough.

ORGANIC FLOURS: We don't detect flavor or texture differences with organic flour, but if you like organic products, by all means use them (we often do). They're not required, and they certainly cost more. One reason some people take up the bread-baking hobby is to be able to eat organic bread every day, as it is usually unavailable commercially or is prohibitively expensive. There are now a number of organic flour brands available in the supermarket, but the best selection remains at your local organic food co-op, where you can buy it in bulk.

POTATO FLOUR: Cooked and then dehydrated potatoes are ground to a powder to produce flour that helps create bread that has a smooth crumb and stays fresher longer. This flour should not be confused with potato starch, which is a much-whiter powder and has different baking and nutritional properties.

RICE FLOUR: White rice flour is used for its fine texture and its flavor. You'll want to avoid using glutinous rice flour, which has different baking properties.

VITAL WHEAT GLUTEN (sometimes called "wheat gluten flour"): You can boost the strength, stretch, and structure of the whole wheat dough by adding this powdered extract of the wheat's endosperm. Whole grain flours have more germ and bran, but less gluten, so we use one or two teaspoons vital wheat gluten per cup of whole grain flour in some of our breads to improve its performance and increase the storage life of the dough.

Water

Throughout the book, we call for lukewarm water. This means water that feels just a little warm to the touch; if you measured it with a thermometer, it would be no higher than 100°F (38°C). The truth is, we never use a thermometer and we've never had a yeast failure due to excessive temperature—but it can happen, so be careful.

About water sources: We find that the flavors of wheat and yeast overwhelm the contribution of water to bread's flavor, so we use ordinary tap water run through a home water filter, but that's only because it's what we drink at home. Assuming your own tap water tastes good enough to drink, use it filtered or unfiltered; we can't tell the difference in finished bread.

Eggs

All of the recipes in the book were tested with large eggs. The most important thing to know about the eggs is that they should be room temperature when mixed into your dough, or they will chill your dough and the rising time will need to be increased. If your eggs are not room temperature when you go to mix your dough, just stick them (in the shell) in a bowl of very warm (you should still be comfortable touching it) water for about 10 minutes.

Dairy and Nondairy Substitutes

MILK: We typically use whole milk in these doughs, because its added fat lends a richness to the bread. Lower-fat milks will also work. You can also substitute nondairy milk for any of the recipes (rice, almond, coconut, and soy). We recommend going with an unsweetened variety, since many of these breads are already sweet. If you can't find an unsweetened milk substitute, just adjust the sweetener in the recipe by a tablespoon or two, depending on the milk.

SOFT CHEESE: Some of our European breads call for soft cheeses called quark and farmer's cheese. They are considered "curd cheese," like a cross between cottage cheese and cream cheese. If you can't find quark or farmer's cheese (which are sometimes hiding in the dairy case of your grocer), you can use cream cheese, whole milk ricotta, or even a combination of the two.

Fats

BUTTER: Butter is delicious. It is a staple in these breads. We tested the recipes with national brands that are found across the country, but if you can get your hands on a locally made butter, by all means use it. We always call for unsalted butter so that you can control the saltiness of your recipe. If you want to use a butter substitute, just be sure it is suitable for substituting one-for-one with butter. The flavor may be slightly different, but we've had good results with some butter substitutes.

COCONUT OIL: Though vegetable-based, coconut oil is solid at room temperature, so melt it in a microwave or double boiler before using, just like butter. It works well as a substitute for other oils or butter in our recipes, and like other vegetable oils, it's completely vegan. It lends a mild coconut flavor to enriched breads; our taste testers loved it.

GHEE: Ghee is butter that has been clarified and slightly toasted. It is a staple in Indian kitchens because of its wonderful flavor. Since the heat-sensitive milk solids are toasted and then strained off, ghee can be heated to a much higher temperature than regular butter. It can be found in many South Asian markets, but we prefer to make our own. The following recipe will yield 12 ounces (about 1⅔ cups): Melt 1 pound of unsalted butter in a medium saucepan over low heat. When it has completely melted, bring it to a boil and continue until it is frothy. Reduce the heat to low and cook gently, until the milk solids have settled to the bottom of the pot and are golden brown. Strain the ghee through a fine-mesh sieve. Allow it to cool completely, cover, and refrigerate. The ghee will last in the refrigerator for a month.

OILS: Vegetable oil—either blends or pure products made from soybean, safflower, sunflower, peanuts, canola, or corn—are rich in polyunsaturated fat. All work well in our recipes, and they're nice, reasonably priced options. They don't impart any particular flavor to baked breads.

Yeast

Use whatever yeast is readily available; with our approach you just won't be able to tell the difference between the various national brands of yeast (though we tested our recipes with Red Star yeast), nor between packages labeled "granulated," "active dry," "instant," "quick-rise," or "bread machine." Fresh cake yeast works fine as well (though you will have to increase the yeast volume by 50 percent to achieve the same rising speed). The long storage time of our doughs acts as an equalizer between all of those subtly different yeast products. **One strong recommendation: If you bake frequently, buy yeast in bulk or in 4-ounce jars, rather than in packets (which are much less economical).**

Food co-ops often sell yeast by the pound, in bulk (usually the Red Star brand). Make sure that bulk-purchased yeast is fresh by chatting with your co-op manager. Freeze yeast after opening to extend its shelf life, and use it straight from the freezer, or store smaller containers in the refrigerator (use within a few months). Between the two of us, we've had only one yeast failure in many years of baking, and it was with an outdated envelope stored at room temperature. **The real key to avoiding yeast failure is to use liquid that is no warmer than lukewarm (about 100°F). Hot liquid kills yeast.**

USING YEAST PACKETS INSTEAD OF JARRED OR BULK YEAST:
Throughout the book, we call for 1 tablespoon of granulated yeast for 4 pounds of dough. **You can substitute one packet of granulated yeast for a tablespoon, even though, technically speaking, those amounts aren't perfectly equivalent (1 tablespoon is a little more than the 2¼ teaspoons found in one packet).** We've found that this makes little difference in the initial rise time or in the performance of the finished dough.

MODERN YEAST . . . almost never fails if used before its expiration date, so you *do not* need to "proof" the yeast (test for its freshness by demonstrating that it bubbles in sweetened warm water). And you don't have to wait for yeast to fully dissolve after mixing with water. You can even mix all the dry ingredients first, and *then* add liquids.

After several days of high-moisture storage, yeasted dough begins to take on a flavor and aroma that's close to the flavor of natural sourdough starters used in many artisan breads. This flavor is desirable in some bread, but the flavor may be a bit overpowering in a sweet bread, so we recommend freezing any leftover dough before the fermentation gets too strong.

Salt: Adjust It to Your Taste

All of our recipes were tested with Morton brand kosher salt, which is coarsely ground. If you measure salt by volume and you're using something finer or coarser, you need to adjust the amount, because finer salt packs denser in the spoon. The following measurements are equivalent:

> Table salt (fine): 2 teaspoons
> Morton Kosher Salt (coarse): 1 tablespoon
> Diamond Kosher Salt (coarsest): 1 tablespoon plus 1 teaspoon

You can use sea salt, but be sure to adjust for its grind. If it's finely ground, you need to measure it like table salt above, and if it's more coarsely ground than Morton, you'll need to increase the volume accordingly. And save the really expensive artisan sea salts for sprinkling on finished products—artisan salts lose their unique flavors when baked. **If you decide to weigh salt to avoid the problem of compensating for fineness-of-grind, do so only for double batches or larger (see sidebar, page 15).**

In traditional bread recipes, salt is used not only for flavor—it also helps tighten and strengthen the gluten. Because our dough is slack in the first place and is stored for so long, the differences between high- and low-salt versions of our doughs are less pronounced. Adjust the salt to suit your palate and your health. We love the taste of salt

> **A NOTE ABOUT YEAST AND SALT:** In the recipes, we provide weight equivalents for yeast and salt, which is a more professional technique—but professionals measure out enormous batches. Be sure your home scale weighs accurately in the lower ranges; otherwise, spoon-measure yeast and salt.
>
> If you find your dough is too salty or yeasty, you can reduce them. You can reduce the yeast by 1 teaspoon and still get a fast-enough rise, so you don't have to worry about leaving dough with eggs out on the counter too long. It may take an extra hour, but that poses no harm to the dough. The salt you can reduce by half or even eliminate it, although we like the flavor better with some salt. You'll have to experiment with the flavor and see how much salt works for you.

and don't have any health-related salt restrictions. Salt can help bring out flavor, even in sweet dough, but you may find you want to decrease the salt. The low end of our salt range will be salty enough for many—and if health conditions require it, you can decrease salt radically and the recipes will still work. In fact, you can bring the salt all the way down to zero, though the taste and texture will certainly change.

Sweeteners

Sweetness is a key quality of most holiday breads. Holidays are a time to celebrate, and most cultures associate that with serving sweets. Neither of us cares for overly sweet desserts or breads, so in most cases our breads reflect that preference. There are some cases, like Monkey Bread and Caramel Rolls, where sticky sweetness is the whole point, and we gladly indulge.

Granulated Sugars

The recipes may call for white, brown, confectioners' (powdered), and/or raw sugars. You can use standard or organic brands for any of the recipes. We did not test coconut sugar or other sugar sources for these recipes, so you will need to experiment with their sweetness intensity.

WHITE GRANULATED SUGAR: This is the most common sugar, and we're all familiar with its pure white sweetness. Our recipes work equally well with cane and beet sugars, which are the two main types of granulated sugar found in the United States.

BROWN SUGAR AND RAW SUGAR: Like white sugar, these less-refined sugars are made from sugar cane or sugar beets, but they retain trace amounts of the nutrients, color, and flavor found in molasses. Brown sugar can be light or dark, and for our purposes it doesn't matter which one you pick. The color of the brown sugar is determined by how much molasses is added back to the white sugar before packaging. They impart a caramel flavor as well. If you bake with cup measures, you want to be sure to pack the brown sugar into the cup to get the accurate amount. Demerara, muscovado, and turbinado are three types of raw sugar; all have a larger grain than regular brown sugar. Raw sugar is also only used on the top of the loaf. Its larger grains don't mix into the dough quite as well, and it measures differently because of the size of the crystals.

CONFECTIONERS' (POWDERED) SUGAR: We generally only use confectioners' sugar to dust over a bread or in icing recipes for the top of a loaf; we don't bake with it.

Liquid Sweeteners

In some cases, we use liquid sweeteners in the dough instead of granulated sugar to flavor the dough and give it a certain texture. You can really switch back and forth among these sweeteners, even substituting sugar. It will change the flavor and texture slightly, but for some people, the type of sugar used is an important health choice, so do what works for you.

BARLEY MALT: Made from sprouted barley, it is very dark, sweet with malt sugar, and quite thick. It adds a beery, yeasty flavor to bread. Barley malt is the main ingredient in beer, and malt sugar is a great sugar for feeding yeast.

HONEY: This is the liquid sweetener we call for most frequently in the book, produced by busy bees the world over from naturally occurring sugars in the nectar of the flowers that they visit. Honey's flavor is determined by the type of plant nectar the honeybee collects. Some honeys have very intense flavor, such as buckwheat honey, while others are quite mild, such as clover honey. We've had nice results with all kinds of honey, so experiment with different types and see which you prefer.

MAPLE SYRUP: All maple syrup is now labeled grade A, but there are different colors and flavors. Golden, which is lightest in color and mildest in flavor, is the most common and popular. Many consider it the more desirable color, but we actually prefer to use the darker maple syrup, which is made later in the production season and has a stronger flavor. It is great for baking because the flavor stands up to the other ingredients, but either syrup will work nicely.

MOLASSES: Molasses is an unrefined sweetener derived from sugar cane. Blackstrap molasses is the product of three boilings of the sugar cane, so it concentrates the nutrients. Its iron, magnesium, calcium, copper, potassium, and vitamin B_6 content makes it one of the most nutrient-rich sweeteners, more so than molasses that isn't labeled as blackstrap. It is used in recipes to add color and a deep, rich flavor. We find that unsulphured molasses has the best flavor.

Seeds and Nuts

Seeds and nuts are central to the flavor and aesthetics of many holiday breads. The only problem you can run into with seeds or nuts is that the oil inside can go rancid if you keep them too long. Freeze them if you are storing for longer than three months. If they've been stored more than a year, taste a few before using them.

Some of our recipes call for toasting the seeds or nuts first. You can buy them toasted or easily do it yourself by spreading the seeds or nuts out on a baking sheet and baking at 350°F for a short time. The timing will depend on the size of the seeds or nuts, so keep a close eye on them. If you only need a tiny amount, you can also toast them in a dry skillet over medium heat on the stove.

ALMOND PASTE: This thick paste is made of pulverized almonds and sugar. It is a cousin to marzipan and differs only in the amount of sugar added (almond paste has less sugar), so you can really use either one in our recipes. It is used in many recipes throughout the book in the dough and as a filling, both in its pure form and mixed into an almond cream.

Chocolate

Some of our enriched breads call for chocolate—either cocoa powder, bar chocolate, or chunks. You will notice an improvement in flavor and recipe performance if you use the highest-quality chocolate available. For bittersweet bar chocolate, Valrhona is our favorite, but Callebaut, Scharffen Berger, Lindt, Guittard, Ghirardelli, and other premium brands also work quite well. Our favorite unsweetened cocoa powder is Valrhona, but Droste, Ghirardelli, and other premium brands also give good results. In our recipes, it doesn't matter if the cocoa powder is Dutch-processed (alkali-treated) or not: The question of Dutch process is only important for baked goods that rise with baking soda or baking powder—yeast doesn't seem to care. If premium chocolate is unavailable, try the recipes with your favorite supermarket brands of solid chocolate or cocoa. Hershey's Special Dark Cocoa powder (unsweetened) is a terrific product for the money. The premium stuff is not an absolute requirement, by any means.

Extracts and Spices
EXTRACTS: We recommend using pure extracts, since they are made with the natural essence of vanilla, almond, orange, or anything else you are flavoring your breads with. If you use imitation or artificial flavorings, you may introduce a chemical aftertaste to the breads. Only use them if you are used to working with those flavors and are sure you like them.

GROUND SPICES: Once ground, spices can lose their aroma and taste if they are too old, so it is best to grind your own whole spices. The easiest way to do this is in a spice or coffee grinder. A mortar and pestle also works and is a rather relaxing exercise.

SAFFRON: These aromatic threads come from the crocus flower and lend an earthy, almost hay-like, flavor and bright yellow color to bread. Saffron is a spice that is fairly common in holiday breads because of its exotic color and probably because it is too expensive to use all year round. This one is for special occasions.

Dried Fruit

We make recommendations, based on tradition, for the type of dried fruits to use in your holiday breads, but they are just suggestions and you should use whatever pleases you. Zoë's eldest son won't touch anything with raisins, so they are avoided at all costs (mostly), and we understand that someone's palate takes precedence over tradition.

Although we try to use naturally dried fruit whenever possible, there are certain fruits, like apricots, that are just prettier when they are dried with preservatives. If you are going for a dramatic color, you may have to go with the brighter fruit.

3

EQUIPMENT

In the spirit of our approach, we've tried to keep our list spare and present items in order of use.

SCALE: We love to weigh our ingredients rather than use measuring cups. It's faster and more accurate, and it's begun to catch on in the United States. Luckily, digital scales are getting cheaper all the time, so we now include weights for ingredients in all our dough recipes. Just press "tare" or "zero" after each ingredient is added to the dough vessel, and you can use these scales without slowing down to do the arithmetic.

The scale is also a consistent way to measure out dough for loaves or flatbreads, but it isn't absolutely necessary because we also give you a visual cue for dough weight (for example, a grapefruit-size piece is 1 pound, and an orange-size piece is about ½ pound of dough).

DRY MEASURING CUPS: Avoid 2-cup dry measuring cups because they are inaccurate when used with the scoop-and-sweep method specified in our recipes. The 2-cup measures collect too much flour due to excessive packing down into the cup. And be sure to use *dry* measuring cups for flour, which allow you to level the top of the cup by sweeping across with a knife; you can't level off a liquid measuring cup filled with flour.

A BUCKET; A LARGE PLASTIC STORAGE CONTAINER; OR A GLASS, STAINLESS-STEEL, OR CROCKERY CONTAINER WITH A LID: You can mix and store the dough in the same vessel—this will save you from washing one more item (it all figures into the five minutes a day). Look for a food-grade container that holds about 6 quarts, to allow for the initial rise. Round containers are easier to mix in than square ones (flour gets caught in corners). Great options are available on our website, or from Tupperware, King Arthur Flour's website, and kitchen-supply specialty stores, as well as discount chains like Costco and Target. Some food-storage buckets include a vented lid, which allows gases to escape during the fermentation process. You can usually close the vent (or seal the lid) after the first two days, because gas production has really slowed by then. If your vessel has a plastic lid, you can poke a tiny hole in the lid to allow gas to escape. Avoid glass or crockery containers that create a truly airtight seal (with a screw top, for example), because trapped gases could shatter them. If you don't have a vented container, just leave the lid open a crack for the first two days of storage.

And of course, you can always use a mixing bowl covered with plastic wrap (don't use a towel; it sticks miserably to high-moisture dough).

STAND MIXER—THIS IS EVEN EASIER THAN HAND-MIXING: You can use a heavy-duty stand mixer, fitted with the paddle attachment, to speed mixing. Some of the doughs in this book are purposefully firm so they'll hold their shape when baked, and they are easier to mix in a stand mixer. A 5-quart-capacity model is large enough; anything smaller will not hold a full batch of our dough. We've found that in larger mixers—6 quarts or larger—the dough hook actually does work better, so, experiment if you're having trouble incorporating the wet and dry ingredients with a paddle. Note that some manufacturers call the paddle attachment the "flat beater." Some readers have reported that, especially with the larger mixers, or when using a rubber-edged paddle attachment (which we don't recommend), dough can "climb up" the mixing attachment and avoid being mixed. If this happens, you can stop the mixer and scrape the paddle and bowl a few times while mixing.

DOUGH WHISK: Unlike flimsy egg-beating whisks, Danish-style dough whisks are made from strong, non-bendable wire on a wood handle, and they're used to blend liquid and dry ingredients together quickly in the dough bucket. We find that they work faster, offer less resistance than a traditional wooden spoon, and are far cooler-looking—although a wooden spoon works fine, too.

KITCHEN SHEARS: You'll need something to cut dough out of the storage bucket, and shears are perfect for the job. You will also need shears to help shape some of the loaves; we recommend a pair with long blades.

ROLLING PIN: We love the skinny French rolling pins that look like large dowels, tapered or straight, but traditional American-style pins with handles work well too and can be easier on the hands. We have tried them all and have determined that wood, marble, and metal all get the job done; we've even rolled out dough with a bottle of wine in a pinch.

DOUGH SCRAPER ("BENCH KNIFE"): A dough scraper makes it easier to work with wet dough—especially when you're first learning our method. It can help prevent things from sticking to the work surface. Just scrape wet dough off the work surface when it sticks—this is particularly useful if working with dough when it's rolled out thin. The scraper is also handy for dividing dough and scraping excess cornmeal or flour off your hot baking stone. We prefer the rigid steel scrapers over the flexible plastic ones—in part because you can't use plastic to scrape off a hot stone.

PARCHMENT PAPER: Use a paper that's temperature-rated to withstand what's called for in your recipe. Parchment is used to line baking sheets and as a sling in your loaf pans, cake pans, and even your crock pot. It makes cleanup easier and in many cases helps to prevent breads from sticking to the pan. Don't use products labeled as pastry parchment, butcher paper, or waxed paper—they smoke and will stick to baked bread dough.

SILICONE MATS: Nonstick, flexible silicone baking mats are convenient and can be reused thousands of times. They're terrific for lower-temperature recipes like sweet brioches and challahs, but we find that flatbreads and other lean-dough specialties don't crisp as well on silicone. They're used on top of a baking sheet and don't need to be greased, so cleanup is a breeze. Be sure to get a mat rated to the temperature you need—they're generally not rated for high-temperature baking.

LOAF PANS: For loaves, we prefer smaller pans with approximate dimensions of 8½ × 4½ inches. This size pan is often labeled as holding 1 pound of dough, but we specify a more generous fill—up to 2 pounds when filled three-quarters full. Loaf pans are made of many materials and we've had great success with them all, but we generally recommend those with a nonstick surface if you have them. Traditional loaf pans (without the nonstick coating) can be more challenging, and if you have had an issue with sticking, we suggest you line your pans with parchment paper. No matter the material, be sure to grease well with butter.

MINI LOAF PANS: For smaller sandwich breads, and especially when baking with kids, it's fun to use mini loaf pans. They're sometimes labeled "number-1" loaf pans, mea-

sure about 6 × 3 inches, and hold about ½ pound of dough. They bake faster than full-size loaf pans, so check for doneness sooner than the recipe calls for when using them.

CAKE PANS: For several of our breads, we recommend baking in cake pans. The pans that work the best have straight sides that are 2 or 3 inches tall. These pans produce a beautiful bread, and their height ensures that any caramel or other filling won't escape while baking. If you don't have tall pans, you will want to bake in a larger pan than specified; for instance, if a recipe calls for a tall 8-inch pan, you can bake in a short 9-inch pan.

Springform pan: There are a few recipes that will bake best in a springform pan, for easy removal, but you can also carefully invert them out of a regular cake pan if you don't have a springform.

Bundt pan: Some of our holiday breads look the most festive, and bake the best, in a fluted Bundt pan.

Kugelhopf pan: This is a tall, narrow pan that looks a lot like a Bundt, but has a more elegant profile. You can bake a kugelhopf bread in a Bundt, but it won't have quite the same classic look.

PAN MATERIALS

Metal pans come in several colors of metal, and they produce different results. The darker the pan, the darker the crust will be, because it conducts more heat to the bread. If you want a paler crust, try a light metal pan. The gold-colored metal pans are right in the middle.

Ceramic pans are great and produce a lovely bread, but you need to make sure they are well greased or even lined with parchment paper to prevent the breads from sticking.

Silicone pans also work well, but even though they are made of a nonstick material, we found that greasing them is essential. The crust tends to come out on the light side.

We didn't test these breads in **cast-iron pans**, but they would likely work as well. Just be aware that the crust will come out darker, and you will probably want to line them with parchment paper.

BRIOCHE PAN: Traditionally, brioche is baked either in a fluted brioche mold or in a loaf pan. The fluted mold is easy to find either online or in any baking supply store. See sidebar on pan materials (page 26).

PANETTONE MOLDS: Traditional panettone is made in a tall, cylindrical pan with a removable bottom, making it easier to remove the bread. If you can't find an authentic panettone pan, you can use ceramic ramekins lined with parchment. If your pan doesn't have a removable bottom, you will need to line it with parchment paper to easily remove the bread, or you can buy decorative panettone molds made from paper that serve as the pan and gift wrap. You can also bake smaller panettones in muffin papers; we chose a tulip-shaped liner for ours (see page 222).

HEAVY-GAUGE BAKING SHEETS, JELLY-ROLL PANS, AND COOKIE SHEETS: The highest-quality baking sheets are made of super-heavyweight aluminum and have short rims (sometimes called jelly-roll pans). When lined with parchment paper or a silicone mat, they are our preferred baking surface. We prefer lining them to greasing, because it saves on clean up and the bottom of the bread doesn't brown quite as much.

An "air-insulated" baking sheet can add a bit of protection so that your bottom crust won't get too dark—you can also achieve this by stacking two baking sheets together. Thin cookie sheets can be used, but they are more likely to warp and they may also scorch bottom crusts due to their uneven heat delivery.

PIZZA PEEL: This is a flat board with a long handle used to slide bread or flatbreads onto a hot stone. Wood or metal work well. Prepare the peel with cornmeal, flour, or parchment paper before putting dough on it, or everything will stick to it, and possibly to your stone. If you don't have a pizza peel, a flat cookie sheet without sides will do, but it will be more difficult to handle. A wood cutting board also works in a pinch—some have handles that make them almost as easy to work with as peels.

PASTRY BRUSHES: These are used to paint egg wash, butter, or water onto the surface of the loaf just before baking. We prefer the natural-bristle style to the silicone, but that's a matter of taste.

ZESTER: Many of the holiday breads in this book call for citrus zest. Depending on how strong you want the flavor, you can use a Microplane zester, which produces a fine zest without getting much of the bitter pith, or use a coarser zester when you want an assertive citrus flavor. We will make recommendations in the recipes, but you decide which suits your taste.

THERMOMETERS:

Oven thermometer: Home ovens are often off by up to 75 degrees, so this is an important item. You need to know the actual oven temperature to get predictable bread-baking results. An inexpensive oven thermometer (less than twenty dollars) will help you get results just like the ones you see in our pictures. Place your oven thermometer right on the rack or stone for best results. A hot oven drives excess water out of wet dough, but if it's too hot you'll burn the crust before fully baking the crumb (the bread's interior). Too low, and you'll end up with a pale crust and under-cooked crumb unless you extend the baking time—but that can give you a thick, hard crust. Without the thermometer, your bread baking will have an annoying element of trial and error. If your oven runs significantly hot or cool, you may want to have it recalibrated by a professional. Otherwise, just compensate by adjusting your heat setting.

When a baking stone is in place, your oven may take 30 to 60 minutes to preheat. And digital oven settings are no more accurate than old-fashioned dial displays, so rely on your oven thermometer. If you don't like the result you're getting with a 30-minute preheat, consider a longer one (45 to 60 minutes).

Candy thermometer: You will need one of these for making doughnuts. We like the

Taylor thermometer that hangs flat against the pot of oil. If you are comfortable using an instant-read thermometer, that will also work.

EQUIPMENT FOR BAKING WITH STEAM (You Only Need One of These): There aren't that many recipes in this book that require steam, but if they do, you have options.

> **1. Metal broiler tray to hold boiling water for steam:** This is our first choice for creating steam when needed to achieve a crispy crust. Pour hot tap water (or drop a handful of ice cubes) into the preheated broiler tray just before closing the oven door. Do not use a glass pan to catch water for steam, or it will shatter on contact with the water!

Some ovens (including most professional-style ones and many that heat with gas) don't have a good seal for holding in steam, so try one of these alternatives:

> **2. Food-grade water sprayer:** Spray the oven with several spritzes of water as soon as you put the bread in the oven. Open the door and spray it at 30-second intervals for two more sprayings.

> **3. Metal bowl or aluminum-foil roasting pan for covering loaves in the oven:** By trapping steam next to the loaf as it bakes, you can create the humid environment that produces a crisp crust. The bowl or dish needs to be heat-tolerant and tall enough that the rising loaf won't touch it, but not so large that it hangs beyond the edge of the stone, or it won't trap the steam. After 15 minutes of baking, remove the bowl to brown the crust.

BAKING STONE, STEEL, CAST-IRON, OR UNGLAZED QUARRY TILES: For breads that have a crust, they'll turn out crisper when baked on one of these, especially in combination with a steam environment (see above). Thick stones take longer to preheat compared to thinner ones, or to steel or cast iron. Unglazed quarry tiles, available from home-improvement stores, are inexpensive and work well. You'll need several of them to line an oven shelf.

BREAD KNIFE: A serrated bread knife does a great job of cutting through fresh bread without tearing or compressing. It's the best implement we've found for slashing high-moisture loaves just before baking. A razor blade and French *lame* (pronounced "lamm") are also great tools for slashing the dough.

COOLING RACKS: Cooling racks are fashioned of wire or other thin metal and are usually intended for cake. They are very helpful in preventing the soggy bottom crust that can result when you cool bread on a plate or other nonporous surface.

CROCK POT: Many of these recipes can be made in a crock pot. There are obvious limitations on size and shape, but you can get a wonderful loaf from your slow cooker and never turn on the oven. Any shape and size will work, but it will determine how much dough you can use and what shape the finished loaf will be. All machines run differently and can range in power, so you will need to monitor your first loaf closely to make sure it isn't "baking" too quickly and burning on the bottom. We found that baking on high power worked great, but you may find your crock pot runs hotter and a lower setting is needed. Some machines require some kind of liquid in the pot to prevent the ceramic vessel from cracking, so check with the manufacturer before using yours.

CONVECTION OVEN: A convection oven can produce a first-rate brown and crispy crust, and speeds baking by circulating hot air around bread. It may take a couple times to get the timing perfect. Some older convection models specify that temperatures should be lowered 25 degrees to prevent overbrowning, while many recent models make the correction automatically, so check your manual. In some, you'll need to turn the loaf around at the halfway point so that each side will brown evenly.

These instructions apply only to range-based convection ovens, not microwaves with convection modes, which we have not tested.

4

TIPS AND TECHNIQUES

This chapter will help you perfect your holiday and celebration breads. In the discussion that follows, we provide tips and techniques for creating professional-quality breads. We like to put this information right up front, so you know you have a resource for any questions that may come up. If there are issues we don't cover here, please ask us on BreadIn5.com.

Measuring Ingredients by Weight Rather than Cup Measures

Many readers of our first books, especially those outside the United States, asked us for weight equivalents. Using a scale is the quickest and most accurate way to mix up a batch of dough.

Using digital scales (see Equipment, page 21): Digital scales are a snap to use. Simply press the "tare" (zeroing) button after placing your empty mixing vessel on the scale. Then "tare" again before adding each subsequent ingredient. There's less cleanup, and your measurements won't be affected by different scooping styles, or how tightly or loosely compacted your ingredient was.

Weighing small-quantity ingredients: Since most scales for home use are accurate only to the nearest ⅛ of an ounce (3 or 4 grams), measuring small amounts this way introduces inaccuracy—this becomes less important when measuring larger quantities for doubled recipes. **Unless you're confident of your scale's accuracy for very small amounts, or you're making a double batch or larger, measure salt, yeast, and spices with measuring spoons.**

Mixing

All of these recipes can be mixed by hand with either a wooden spoon or a Danish dough whisk (see page 23); however, we did find that using a stand mixer, if you have one, makes mixing some of them an easier task. Because many of these breads are based on traditional shapes, we found it much easier to achieve the look with a stiffer dough. One of the greatest benefits of our wet dough from previous books was that the longer the dough was stored, the wetter it was. Since these doughs need to be frozen after five days, it isn't as beneficial to have them so wet. As a result, the dough can be a bit drier and may not come together as easily with a hand-held tool. If you do not have a stand mixer or just don't want to dirty another container, you may just need to use your hands to make sure these doughs are thoroughly mixed.

Avoiding Strong Fermentation Flavor

Some people detect a yeasty or alcohol aroma or flavor in the dough, and that's no surprise—yeast multiplies in dough, creating alcohol and carbon dioxide gas as it ferments sugars and starches. Stored dough develops these sourdough-like flavors, and most people appreciate them in our lean doughs. But it isn't always a desired characteristic in a sweet dough. We specify the amount of time a dough can be stored in the refrigerator before a too-strong flavor develops, but if you happen to be sensitive to the alcohol flavor (some people detect it long before others), here are some things to try:

1. Always vent the rising container as directed, especially in the first two days of storage (see page 22). You can even poke a tiny hole in the lid to allow gas to escape.

2. Consider using less yeast. Since many of these doughs have eggs, we need the dough to rise at a relatively quick rate, but you can decrease the yeast by 1 teaspoon per full batch. This may increase the rising time by an hour.

3. Store your dough for shorter periods than we specify, freezing the remainder. Or make smaller batches so they're used up more quickly.

WHAT ARE "LEAN" AND "ENRICHED" DOUGHS?

"Lean" doughs are those made without significant amounts of eggs, fat, dairy, or sweetener. They bake well without burning or drying out at high temperatures. Doughs "enriched" with lots of eggs, fat, dairy, or sweeteners generally require a lower baking temperature (and a longer baking time), because eggs and sweeteners burn at high temperatures.

Storing Dough to Save Time and Develop Flavor

Depending on the type of dough you are making, the amount of time you can store it will be different. In this book, the recipes are mostly enriched with butter, sweeteners, milk, and/or eggs, so the amount of time you can store them in the refrigerator is shorter than you may be used to in our previous books. The enriched doughs, due to the additional sugar, tend to ferment at a faster rate, which means that you need to use the dough or freeze it before it tastes too strong. The eggs and dairy also make it impossible to store for as long in the refrigerator. To make a big batch and be able to store the dough, we recommend that you freeze the dough after the suggested refrigerator storage time. This still saves the time of mixing up fresh dough for each loaf, but ensures that your bread will taste great.

A few of the doughs (lean dough) in this book are still based on dough that can be stored for up to fourteen days in the refrigerator. Sourdough flavor develops over the lifespan of the batch. That means that your first loaves won't taste the same as your last ones.

How much to make and store: Your initial time investment (mixing the dough) is the most significant one, though it generally takes no more than fifteen minutes. By mixing larger batches, you can spread that investment over more days of bread making. So, we recommend mixing enough dough to make at least two large loaves or several smaller ones. For larger households or to give as gifts, that might mean doubling or even tripling the recipe. Don't forget to choose a container large enough to accommodate the rising of the larger batch.

Dough Consistency: How Wet Is Wet Enough, but Not Too Wet?

Our recipes were carefully tested, and we arrived at the ratio of wet to dry ingredients with an eye toward creating a relatively slack dough. But flours can vary in their protein content, the degree to which they're compacted into their containers, and in the amount of water they've absorbed from the environment. And the environment changes; in most places, humidity will fluctuate over the course of the year. All of this means that our recipes may produce slightly variable results depending on humidity, compaction, and the flour brand you're using.

The doughs in this book are even more forgiving than the ones in our previous books. If your dough is stiff or loose, it will still produce a wonderful bread. Because we are not going for the open-crumb structure of an artisan baguette, with its characteristically big holes, and most of these breads are meant to have a tight, uniform interior, it is really okay for them to be a little wetter or drier than what we intended.

However, if they're too loose and wet, and don't hold a shape well or are too difficult to shape into a braid or other form, increase the flour, by 2 tablespoons at a time, in your next batch. If you don't want to wait until you mix up another batch, you can work extra flour into a too-wet dough (it's easiest to do this in a stand mixer and give it some time to absorb after doing this). For too-dry batches (which can happen, when using cup measures or in the dry winter), it can be challenging to mix water into the dough—but it can be done. We highly recommend using a stand mixer with the dough hook attachment if you have to add water to the dough, and do it in 1-tablespoon additions. Once the gluten has formed in the dough, it is a bit too stretchy and difficult to mix by hand. If all else fails, overly wet dough still works well in loaf pans.

Conversion Tables for Liquid Measures and Oven Temperatures

VOLUMES

U.S. SPOON AND CUP MEASURES	U.S. LIQUID VOLUME	METRIC VOLUME
I teaspoon	⅓ ounce	5 ml
I tablespoon	½ ounce	15 ml
¼ cup	2 ounces	60 ml
½ cup	4 ounces	120 ml
I cup	8 ounces	240 ml
2 cups	16 ounces	475 ml
4 cups	32 ounces	950 ml

OVEN TEMPERATURE: FAHRENHEIT TO CELSIUS CONVERSION

DEGREES FAHRENHEIT	DEGREES CELSIUS
350	180
375	190
400	200
425	220
450	230
475	240
500	250
550	288

Preparing the Pan—Butter and/or Parchment Paper

There are so many types of pans to bake in, and we discuss them at length in the equipment chapter (pages 24–27), but our recommended ways to prepare them is pretty straightforward. If you are using a loaf pan with straight sides (as opposed to a fluted pan or Bundt pan), butter the sides and bottom generously and then line the bottom and sides of the pan with a sheet of parchment paper (see page 24) for extra insurance that it will come out cleanly, especially if the bread has sticky ingredients. We find that oil doesn't work as well to prevent sticking, and it certainly doesn't taste as good. These breads are pretty decadent, so we're not sure this is the place to get concerned about using extra butter. If you are using a fluted pan such as a Bundt pan, then generously butter the pan. We also highly recommend nonstick pans if you have them. You will notice that in some cases we even suggest flouring the pan, like you would a cake, for extra insurance that the bread will turn out of the pan cleanly.

Resting Dough Tips

Compared with traditional doughs, our breads get more of their total rise from "oven spring" (the sudden expansion of gases inside the loaf that occurs on contact with hot oven air and baking stone)—and less from "proofing" (the resting time after a loaf is shaped, before baking). So don't be surprised if you don't see as much rising during our resting step as you might with traditional recipes. You'll still get a nice rise from oven spring. If you want to coax a little more rise during the resting period, try prolonging it (see "Resting and Baking Times Are Approximate," page 37). And make sure your oven's the right temperature by checking with a thermometer (see page 28). If the oven is too cool or too hot, you won't get proper oven spring.

After frozen doughs have been defrosted, they may need a longer rest because some of the yeast will not be as active. After a dough has been frozen for a couple of weeks, it may not have the rising strength it did originally, so it may need a slightly longer rest before it is fully ready to bake.

Resting and Baking Times Are Approximate

All of our resting and baking times are approximate. Since loaves are formed by hand, their size will vary from loaf to loaf, which means their resting and baking time requirements can vary. In general, flat or skinny loaves don't need much resting time and will bake rapidly. High-domed loaves will require longer resting and baking times. So, unless you're weighing out exact one-pound loaves and forming the same shapes each time, your resting and baking times will vary, and our listed times should be seen only as a starting point. In general, these breads are lighter and fluffier if you can give them a long rest, up to two hours in some cases. Having said that, they will still be delicious if you need to rush them a tiny bit and cheat the full rest.

For this book on holiday and celebration breads, the longer rest will give you a softer crumb and a loftier result. This is even more important when you are using whole grains in the loaf, which can make a loaf denser.

Because of the longer resting times of many of these loaves, and especially if your environment is particularly dry, we recommend covering the loaf with plastic wrap or a roomy overturned bowl—this prevents the surface from drying out and forming a crust that might constrain rising and oven spring. Skinny or small loaves or flatbreads do well with the shorter resting times; in fact, many flatbreads need none at all (for more on pizza and flatbread, see **Artisan Pizza and Flatbread in Five Minutes a Day**, 2011). Here are some guidelines for varying resting and baking times:

Increase resting and/or baking time if any of the following apply:

- The temperature of your kitchen is low: This only affects rising and resting times, not baking.
- You're baking a larger loaf: A 2-pound white loaf takes at least a 90-minute resting time and 45 to 50 minutes to bake. A 3-pound loaf will take about 2 hours' resting time and nearly an hour to bake.
- You're using more whole grain flour than we call for in the recipe.

A good rule of thumb for resting time after shaping: if you want loaves to develop maximum rise, wait until the dough no longer feels dense and cold. A perfectly rested loaf will begin to feel "jiggly" when you shake it—like set Jell-O.

Baking Tips

Loaves Spread Sideways

Since our dough is wet, it can have less structure than traditional dough. If your loaf spreads instead of rising up during baking, the usual cause is either a dough that is too wet (see page 34) or insufficient "gluten-cloaking," the stretching of the outside of the dough around itself during the shaping step. See our videos on YouTube.com/Bread-In5, and be sure to use enough dusting flour when you shape loaves.

And if your dough is nearing or exceeding the end of its storage life, consider using it in a loaf pan—those don't need as much structure.

Underbaking Issues

The bread is domed when it emerges from the oven, but it softens and seems to collapse as it comes to room temperature: The bread is underbaked. This is most often a problem with large breads, but it can happen with any loaf. As you gain experience, you'll be able to judge just how brown and firm the loaf must be when it is fully baked to prevent this problem with any given loaf size.

The loaf has a soggy or gummy crumb (interior):
- Check your oven temperature with a thermometer (see page 28).
- Make sure you are allowing the dough to rest for the full time period we've recommended. If you don't rest the dough long enough, it will remain dense and will not bake as well or as quickly.
- Your dough may benefit from being a little drier. For the next batch, increase the flour by 2 tablespoons (or decrease the liquids a little) and check the result.
- If you're baking a large loaf (more than two pounds) or it is chock-full of fillings, rest and bake it longer (see page 37).

Don't slice or eat loaves when they're still warm, unless they're flatbreads, rolls, or very skinny loaves. The proteins continue to cook and set as the bread cools. Warm bread has a certain romance, so we know that it's hard to wait for it to cool. But waiting will improve the texture—loaf breads are at their peak of flavor and texture about two hours after they come out of the oven (or whenever they completely cool). Hot or warm bread cuts poorly (the slices collapse) and dries out quickly. Use a sharp, serrated bread knife to go right through the crust and soft crumb. Flatbreads, rolls, and skinny loaves and braids are different—their size makes them easier to bake through despite the high-moisture dough, so you can enjoy them warm.

The top crust won't brown or crisp:

- Achieving a nice, brown top crust isn't typically as much of a problem with breads that are made with sugars or milk, since they tend to naturally caramelize. But if you want a really dramatic caramel-colored top to your loaf, we recommend using an egg wash. But which one? See "Egg Wash—Many Ways" (page 40) for your options.

- For breads that require a baking stone (see page 29), you'll want to preheat it for up to 60 minutes, depending on the thickness of the stone, in an oven whose temperature has been checked with a thermometer.

- Bake with steam when called for. Use one of the methods described on page 29.

- Try the shelf switcheroo for crisp crust: If you're a crisp-crust fanatic, here's the ultimate approach for baking the perfect crust. Place the stone on the bottom shelf and start the loaf there. Two-thirds of the way through baking, transfer the loaf from the stone directly to the top rack of the oven (leave the stone where it is). Top crusts brown best near the top of the oven, and bottom crusts brown best near the bottom. For loaf pan breads, just pop the bread out of the pan before transferring to the top shelf—it makes a big difference.

EGG WASH—MANY WAYS: There are so many ways to make egg wash, and they have different effects. If you want a super-rich caramel color to your loaf, you'll want to use an egg yolk–only wash. You can mix it with cream for an even more dramatic color, or just stick to water. If you're into a super-outrageous finish, you can even add a pinch of sugar or honey. If you want a nice, deep color, but not as dark, a whole-egg wash will achieve the best results. Again, you can decide between cream and water to mix it with. Finally, if you are looking for a shine, but not a deep color, you'll want to use an egg white–only wash, mixed with just water. In all cases, you will mix the egg, yolk, or white with 1 tablespoon of liquid and whisk well with a fork to break up the egg, so you don't end up having bits of egg cooked on your bread.

Overbrowning

We like our breads with some color, but sometimes the breads don't bake evenly and one part of your bread may seem too dark, while other parts are still underbaked. You may want to check the oven for hot spots with an oven thermometer. If your bread is baking unevenly, be sure to rotate it in the oven, which will help color it evenly. If that isn't doing the trick, use a tent. A sheet of foil loosely draped over the spots that are too dark will protect them from further darkening while the rest of the loaf catches up. If the bottom crust is too dark, try baking on an insulated baking sheet (see page 27).

Dry Interior

The bread may be overbaked. Make sure your oven is calibrated properly using an oven thermometer, and double-check your baking time.

Dry blobs of flour in the middle of the loaf: Be sure to completely mix the initial batch, especially if you are mixing by hand. Using wet hands to incorporate the last bits of flour will often take care of this. The culprit is sometimes the shaping step—extra flour can get tucked up under and inside the loaf as it's formed. Use lots of dusting flour, but allow most of it to fall off.

Overly Dense Interior

Your bread is dense, doughy, or heavy:

- Make sure that your dough is not too wet. If you're measuring flour by volume, make sure you are using the scoop-and-sweep method that we describe in Chapter 5, and view our video, "How to Measure Flour," on our YouTube channel (YouTube.com/BreadIn5). And if you're getting inconsistent results, consider weighing the flour using a digital scale rather than measuring it out with measuring cups (see Tips and Techniques, page 31).

- Try a longer rest after shaping, especially if your kitchen is cool or you're making a large loaf: See "Resting and Baking Times Are Approximate," page 37.

- Check your oven temperature with an oven thermometer. If your oven's temperature is off, whether it's too warm or too cool, you won't get proper "oven spring" and the loaf will be dense, with a pale or burnt crust. See Equipment, page 28.

TRY THE "REFRIGERATOR RISE" TRICK: By using the refrigerator, you can shape your dough and then have it rise in the refrigerator for eight to fourteen hours. Simply cut off a piece of dough and shape it as normal. Place the dough on a sheet of parchment or in the required pan, loosely wrap with plastic, and put it back in the refrigerator. **Before baking,** preheat your oven and take the loaf out of the refrigerator. You may find that it has spread slightly and may not have risen much, but it will still have lovely oven spring. Because you don't handle the dough at all after the refrigerator rise, the bubbles in the dough should still be intact. A twenty- to thirty-minute rest on the counter while preheating is all you need, but a longer room-temperature rest will result in a lighter crumb. Then, finish the loaf as directed in the recipe before baking.

Older Dough

For a few of the recipes that have longer refrigerator storage (because they don't have eggs or dairy), especially if you don't bake every day, you may find that toward the end of a batch's life, its entire surface darkens (or even turns gray), and it develops a more intense sourdough flavor; dark liquid may collect. None of this is mold or spoilage—don't toss it; just pour off the liquid and work in enough flour to absorb the excess moisture still in the dough. Then rest the dough for two hours at room temperature before using. If you are not using it right away, refrigerate it again; you can keep it until the end of the dough's recommended life. **Discard any dough that develops mold on its surface, which you can identify as dark or light patches, with or without a fuzzy appearance.**

Freezing Dough

Our dough can be frozen at any point in its batch-life, so long as the initial rise has been completed. It's best to divide it into loaf-sized portions, and then wrap it very well or seal it in airtight containers. Defrost in the refrigerator when ready to use, then shape, rest, and bake as usual. How long to freeze is partly a matter of taste—our dough loses some rising power when frozen, and some people find the results dense if it's frozen for too long. That's especially true for enriched doughs. Here are some basic guidelines for maximum freezing times:

- Lean dough (no eggs and minimal butter or oil): Four weeks
- Enriched dough (eggs, dairy, high amounts of sweeteners or fats): Two to three weeks

Using Up Small Bits of Dough

If you have small amounts of dough left over from several batches, consider baking them all at once. It's a fun way to use up odd-sized pieces of dough. Just form the dough into balls and place them all in a prepared pan together. Let them rise and bake; the times will vary depending on the size of the combined dough balls.

Oddly Shaped Loaves

Your loaves are losing their shape before or after baking:

- Our dough does have a strong oven spring, so loaf breads tend to have a top that cracks open as it rises. We don't mind this rustic look, but if you'd prefer a smooth top, try a much longer rest. This will be especially true if your kitchen is cool. If the dough is not sufficiently rested, it can "explode" into odd shapes, because the yeast is still too active and when it hits the oven, it goes a little bonkers. It won't change the flavor, but it may not have the shape you hoped for.

- If the shaped loaves are losing their form when they bake (braids are splitting), you can let the loaf rest a bit longer and try not braiding it quite so tightly the next time. You can also develop a bit more stretch in the dough by kneading it for a few seconds before shaping (see sidebar page 66).

How to Store Fresh Bread

Most of the breads in this book are enriched and store well wrapped in plastic or foil. If you are not going to finish a loaf in a day or two, it is best to freeze the loaf, since there are no preservatives to extend its shelf life.

We've found that the best way to keep "lean dough" bread fresh once it has been cut is to store it cut-side down on a flat, nonporous surface like a plate or a clean countertop. Don't store inside foil or plastic, which trap humidity and soften the crust by allowing it to absorb water. An exception is pita bread, which is supposed to have a soft crust and can be stored in a plastic bag or airtight container once cooled.

Breads made with whole grains, and those made with dough that has been well aged, stay fresh longest. Use stale bread for making bread crumbs in the food processor, or try one of our recipes like bread puddings (pages 327 and 329), or Bostock (page 330).

High-Altitude Baking

There can be a big difference in how yeast behaves if you live at high altitudes. With less air pressure constraining the rising dough, it balloons up too quickly and then collapses abruptly, giving you a dense result. The following adjustments can help you avoid that by slowing down the initial rise (the dough won't be ready for the refrigerator in the usual 2 hours). If you are having an issue, try these things:

- Decrease the yeast by half or even more.
- Assuming you like the flavor and aren't on a salt-restricted diet, consider a saltier dough—salt inhibits fast yeast growth. And decrease the sugar if there's any in the recipe—it feeds yeast.
- Do the initial dough rise overnight in the refrigerator (also see the refrigerator-rise trick, Tips and Techniques, page 41), and consider mixing the dough using cold liquids.

These techniques allow the dough to rise more slowly, giving it more time to achieve full height without collapsing.

Shipping Breads as Holiday Gifts

Our first recommendation is that you send a copy of our book and maybe a Danish dough whisk as a gift, and have your loved ones bake fresh bread at home. We're kind of kidding, but it really is best to have a loaf come from the oven, perfuming the air with freshly baked bread. Having said that, it is also lovely to receive a gift of home-made bread at the holidays. The loaves in this book are particularly suited to packing and shipping. Breads with a high proportion of fats and sugar tend to have a longer shelf life.

How to ship: Bake the bread, cool it completely, and wrap it very well in plastic to lock in the moisture. You can find decorative plastic bags if you want to be fancy, or just use a large zip lock bag. If you won't be shipping the bread that day, then freeze it until you ship. If you are going to ship it the same day, then swaddle it in bubble wrap or something to prevent it from sliding around a well-fitted box. If you can swing it, ship the box next-day air, so that it is as fresh as possible.

5

THE MASTER RECIPE

There's just no substitute for the nostalgic and comforting taste of a classic white bread. This recipe is perfect for re-creating the lunchbox sandwiches of childhood, only better, or making a golden-brown slice of toast with butter and jam. Just indulgent enough to be a treat, but simple enough to serve at any meal, this bread is sure to be an all-around family favorite.

We chose this classic as the Master Recipe of our book because it's so universal and straightforward. If you aren't familiar with our method, we suggest you start here and get to know our technique in a bit more detail. In this recipe, we'll go through our simple procedure in more depth than you'll find throughout the rest of the book. You will also find great information in our Tips and Techniques chapter.

White Bread Master Recipe

Makes enough dough for two 2-pound loaves. The recipe is easily doubled or halved.

INGREDIENT	VOLUME (U.S.)	WEIGHT (U.S.)	WEIGHT (METRIC)
Lukewarm water (100°F or below)	3 cups	1 pound, 8 ounces	680 grams
Granulated yeast[1]	1 tablespoon	0.35 ounce	10 grams
Kosher salt[1]	1 tablespoon	0.6 ounce	17 grams
Sugar	⅓ cup	3 ounces	85 grams
Oil	¼ cup	2 ounces	58 grams
All-purpose flour	7½ cups	2 pounds, 5½ ounces	1,065 grams
Egg wash (1 egg beaten with 1 tablespoon water) for brushing the loaf			

[1]Can decrease to taste (see pages 15 and 33).

1. Mixing the dough: Mix the yeast, salt, sugar, and oil with the water in a 6-quart, lidded (not airtight) container (see Equipment, Chapter 3, page 22) or a 5-quart stand mixer bowl.

2. Mix in the flour—kneading is unnecessary: Add all of the flour at once, measuring it with dry-ingredient measuring cups or by weighing the ingredients. If you measure

WEIGHING YOUR INGREDIENTS: We include weight equivalents for all our dough recipes, because many of our testers found it was easier to weigh ingredients than to use cup measures. Use a digital scale—they're becoming less expensive all the time. Simply press the "tare" (zeroing) button before adding an ingredient, and then "tare" again to add the next ingredient.

with cups, use the scoop-and-sweep method (see sidebar). Mix with a Danish dough whisk, a wooden spoon or a heavy-duty stand mixer (with paddle) until the mixture is uniform. If you're hand-mixing and it becomes too difficult to incorporate all the flour with the spoon, you can reach into your mixing vessel with wet hands and press the mixture together. Don't knead! It isn't necessary. You're finished when everything is uniformly wet, without dry patches. This step is done in a matter of minutes, and will yield a dough that is fairly tacky.

THE SCOOP-AND-SWEEP METHOD: It's easier to scoop and sweep if you store your flour in a bin rather than the bag it's sold in; it can be hard to get the measuring cups into the bag without making a mess. Gently scoop up the flour with the dry measuring cup, then sweep the top level with a knife or spatula; don't press down into the flour as you scoop or you'll throw off the measurement by compressing. **Don't use an extra-large 2-cup-capacity measuring cup,** which allows the flour to overpack and measures too much flour.

OTHER TOOLS TO USE FOR THE INITIAL MIXING: If you're mixing by hand, a **Danish dough whisk** (page 23) is an effective alternative to a wooden spoon, because it's not a flat, solid surface, it moves more easily through the dough. It's much stouter than a flimsy egg-beating whisk, and it incorporates the wet and dry ingredients in no time flat.

3. Allow to rise: Cover with a lid that fits the container well but isn't completely airtight. If you're using a bowl, cover loosely with plastic wrap. Towels don't work—they stick to wet dough. Lidded (or even vented) plastic buckets are readily available (page 22). Allow the mixture to rise at room temperature for about 2 hours, depending on the room's temperature and the initial water temperature— then refrigerate it and use for up to 7 days. If your container isn't vented, allow gases to escape by leaving it open a crack for the first couple of days in the fridge—after that you can usually close it, but a vented container is best. You can use a portion of the dough any time after the 2-hour rise. Fully refrigerated dough is less sticky and is easier to work with than dough at room temperature, so the first time you try our method, it's best to refrigerate the dough overnight (or at least 3 hours) before shaping a loaf. Once refrigerated, the dough will seem to have shrunk back upon itself and it will never rise again in the bucket—that's normal. **No need to punch down this dough!**

4. On baking day, grease an 8½ × 4½-inch nonstick loaf pan with butter (grease heavily if you are not using a nonstick pan). Dust the surface of the refrigerated dough with flour and, using kitchen shears or a serrated knife, cut off a 2-pound (cantaloupe-size) piece. Dust with more flour and quickly shape it into a ball (form a gluten cloak, see sidebar, page 51) by stretching the surface of the dough around to the bottom, rotating the ball a quarter-turn as you go.

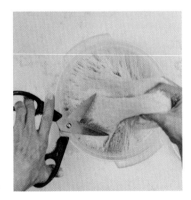

WHAT'S A "GLUTEN CLOAK"? Just imagine a warm blanket being pulled around you on a cold night. Or, for the more technically inclined: what you are trying to do here is to add enough flour to the surface so it can be handled and the protein strands in the surface can be aligned, creating a resilient "cloak" around the mass of wet dough. Visualize a cloak being pulled around the dough, so that the entire ball is surrounded by a skin. See our YouTube channel for a video of the gluten-cloak step (YouTube.com/BreadIn5). Creating this cloak will create a uniform ball and will help the dough from spreading while it rests.

Most of the dusting flour will fall off; it's not intended to be incorporated into the dough. The bottom of the loaf may appear to be a collection of bunched ends, but it will flatten out and adhere during resting and baking. The correctly shaped loaf will be smooth and cohesive. The entire process should take no more than 20 to 40 seconds.

5. Elongate the ball into an oval and drop it, seam side down, into the prepared pan.

Visit BreadIn5.com, where you'll find recipes, photos, videos, and instructional material.

51

RELAX! You don't need to monitor doubling or tripling of volume as with traditional recipes.

6. Cover loosely with plastic wrap and allow to rest at room temperature for **90 minutes.** You may not see much rise during this period; much more rising will occur during baking (oven spring). If you are using fresh dough, that has not been refrigerated, you only have to let it rise for 45 minutes.

7. Preheat the oven to 350°F, with a rack placed in the center of the oven.

8. Brush the top of the loaf with egg wash (see sidebar, page 40).

9. Bake for about 50 minutes, or until medium golden brown and well set. (White bread will not form a hard, crackling crust.) Remove from pan. If the loaf sticks, wait 10 minutes and it will steam itself out of the pan. Allow to cool completely (about 2 hours), preferably on a wire cooling rack, for best flavor, texture, and slicing. Cutting into a hot loaf is tempting, but it won't slice well and may seem underbaked if you break into it before it's cooked.

10. Store the remaining dough in the refrigerator in your lidded or loosely plastic-wrapped container and use it over the next 7 days. If you store your dough in the mixing container, you'll avoid some cleanup. Cut off and shape more loaves as you need them. We often have several types of dough stored in our refrigerators at once. The dough can also be frozen in 2-pound portions in an airtight container for about 3 weeks and defrosted in the refrigerator before use (see page 42).

ADJUSTING THE RESTING TIME:

- Lengthen the resting time if your fridge or the room is particularly cold, if you're making larger loaves, or if your dough has been frozen for more than a week (see page 42 for freezing dough). You can go as long as 2 hours for a 2-pound loaf. Cover the loaf with plastic wrap—it won't stick if the surface is well dusted or under a roomy, over-turned bowl. Don't use a damp towel or it will stick.
- Shorten the resting time by half if you're using fresh, unrefrigerated dough.

INSTANT-READ THERMOMETERS: We're not in love with internal-temperature food thermometers, usually sold as "instant-read" thermometers (as opposed to oven thermometers, which we love, see page 28). They have a pointed probe that you stick into the bread to see if it's reached a target temperature. We find that the inexpensive ones (under $20) aren't all that "instant," and the truly instant (and accurate) digital units cost much more. If you have confidence in your thermometer and your technique, here are some guidelines for fully baked bread:

- Enriched dough (eggs, dairy, butter, sugar): 180°F to 185°F (82°C to 85°C)
- Lean dough (no eggs or dairy): 205°F to 210°F (96°C to 99°C)

Crock Pot Bread (Fast Bread in a Slow Cooker)

Everyone loves crock pots, bubbling away with Swedish meatballs, no-peek chicken, or chili. Over the years we've had requests for a method for baking our dough in one. Bread in a crock pot? We had our doubts, lots of them. We didn't think the slow cooker could get hot enough, thought it would take too long, and didn't think it would bake through or have a nice crust. So we resisted trying it, convinced it would fail. Oh, how wrong we were. The crock pot does indeed get hot enough, and it can take less time than using your oven (depending on your machine) because the rising time is included in the baking. Straight out of the pot, the crust is soft and quite pale, but just a few minutes under the broiler and you get a gorgeous loaf. During the holidays, the oven is prime real estate and it's often too hard to find space to bake bread, so this is the perfect way to get everything done without having to have NASA-like scheduling. Also try Challah (page 147) and Cinnamon Rolls (page 185) in your slow cooker. It's a great way to impress your co-workers by having fresh bread baking under your desk. Jeff actually does this at his day job. True story!

Makes I Crock Pot bread

> I pound (grapefruit-size portion) White Bread Master Recipe dough (page 48)
>   or any other dough in the book
>   All-purpose flour, for dusting

1. To bake: Dust the surface of the refrigerated dough with flour and cut off a 1-pound (grapefruit-size) piece. Dust with more flour and quickly shape it into a ball by stretching the surface of the dough around to the bottom, rotating the ball a quarter-turn as you go.

2. Place the dough on a lightly floured piece of parchment paper and lower the dough into a 4-quart crock pot. Be sure to follow the manufacturer's instructions for proper use.

3. Turn the temperature to high and put on the cover. **(Not all crock pots behave the same, so you should keep an eye on the loaf after about 45 minutes to make sure it is not overbrowning on the bottom or not browning at all. You may need to adjust the time or temperature according to your machine.)**

4. Bake for 1 hour (this will depend on your crock pot; you may need to increase or decrease the time). To check for doneness, it should feel firm when you gently poke the top of the loaf with your finger.

5. The bottom crust should be nice and caramel colored, but the top of the loaf will be quite soft and pale. Some folks desire a softer crust, so they'll love this loaf.

6. You can place the bread under the broiler for 5 minutes or until it is the color you like, with a rack positioned in the middle of the oven.

7. Let the loaf cool completely before serving.

CHECK WITH YOUR CROCK POT'S MANUFACTURER BEFORE TRYING THIS (see page 30.)

Pullman Sandwich Loaf

The beauty of a pullman loaf is its perfectly square slices (see page 80). The dough is baked in a pan with a lid, so it is forced into a neat and clean shape. This uniform style of bread was developed by the Pullman Company (of railroad car fame) to be baked in its compact kitchens and stacked in as little space as possible. It makes a great sandwich loaf, picture-perfect toast, or almond-slathered Bostock (page 330). Any of our bread doughs will work in this pan, but some rise more than others, so you may have to adjust the amounts.

Makes 1 loaf

> Butter, for greasing the pan
> 2½ pounds (large cantaloupe–size portion) White Bread Master Recipe dough (page 48) or any other dough in the book
> All-purpose flour, for dusting

1. To bake: Grease a 9 × 4 × 4-inch nonstick pullman loaf pan with butter. Dust the surface of the refrigerated dough with flour and cut off a 2½-pound (large cantaloupe-size) piece. Dust with more flour and quickly shape it into a ball by stretching the surface of the dough around to the bottom, rotating the ball a quarter-turn as you go.

2. Elongate the ball into an oval and drop it into the prepared pan. You want to fill the pan about three-quarters full, and then cover the pan with the lid.

3. Allow to rest at room temperature for 1 hour and 45 minutes.

4. Preheat the oven to 350°F, with a rack placed in the center of the oven.

5. Bake for about 50 minutes, remove the lid, and bake for an additional 10 minutes. If it pops up when you remove the lid, quickly replace it and continue to bake with the lid on until it is completely set.

6. Remove the loaf from the pan and allow to cool completely on a rack before slicing; otherwise, you won't get well-cut sandwich slices.

Visit BreadIn5.com, where you'll find recipes, photos, videos, and instructional material.

57

<h1 style="text-align:center">6</h1>

<h1 style="text-align:center">THE BASICS</h1>

These are the doughs that great holiday breads are built on. They can be made into incredible sandwich loaves for the everyday celebration that is school lunch or they can be spun into cinnamon rolls, sticky buns, braids, boats, or monkey bread, just to name a few.

Super Strong Dough

We set out to write books that were super easy and didn't require ingredients that weren't already in pantries. For the most part, we stick to that philosophy but for this dough, we want it to be strong and stretchy to make a sturdy sandwich bread (that makes excellent thick-cut toast), Bagels (page 97), a Family-Size Soft Pretzel (page 101), crusty-chewy Pretzel Buns (page 104), and we use it to make our flaky croissant dough (page 339). The trick is to use bread flour, which has a higher protein content (the protein creates the stretchy gluten). It is a bit stiffer than some of our other doughs, so it holds its shape like a champ. You may not stock bread flour in your pantry, but it is easy to find in the baking aisle of your grocery store.

Makes at least two 1½-pound loaves. The recipe is easily doubled or halved.

INGREDIENT	VOLUME (U.S.)	WEIGHT (U.S.)	WEIGHT (METRIC)
Lukewarm water (100°F or below)	2¾ cups	1 pound, 6 ounces	625 grams
Oil	¼ cup	2 ounces	58 grams
Granulated yeast[1]	1 tablespoon	0.35 ounce	10 grams
Kosher salt[1]	1 tablespoon	0.6 ounce	17 grams
Barley malt syrup or honey	2 tablespoons	1 ounce	30 grams
Bread flour	6½ cups	2 pounds	910 grams

[1]Can decrease (see pages 15 and 33).

1. Mixing and storing the dough: Mix the water, oil, yeast, salt, and malt syrup in a 6-quart bowl or a lidded (not airtight) food container.

2. Mix in the flour without kneading, using a spoon or a heavy-duty stand mixer (with paddle). If you're not using a machine, you may need to use wet hands to incorporate the last bit of flour.

3. Cover (not airtight) and allow to rest at room temperature until the dough rises for 2 hours.

4. The dough can be used immediately after the initial rise, though it is easier to handle when cold. Refrigerate the container and use over the next 14 days.

5. On baking day, grease an 8½ × 4½-inch nonstick loaf pan generously with butter. Dust the surface of the refrigerated dough with flour and cut off a 1½-pound (small cantaloupe–size) piece. Dust the piece with more flour and quickly shape it into a ball by stretching the surface of the dough around to the bottom, rotating the ball a quarter-turn as you go.

6. Place in the prepared pan. Cover loosely with plastic wrap and allow to rest at room temperature for 90 minutes.

7. Preheat the oven to 350°F, with a rack placed in the center of the oven.

8. Brush the top of the loaf with egg wash.

9. Bake for about 45 minutes, or until medium golden brown and well set.

10. Allow to cool on a rack before serving.

Milk Bread (Big and Tall)

There is no rule about how large a loaf can be, and if you want a hearty sandwich, we recommend you go big and tall. It's easy to achieve a big loaf, but to get the height we wanted, we baked this loaf in a pullman pan and left the lid off so it could pop out and make a beautiful, rounded loaf. Obviously, you can use this wonderful dough in a normal loaf pan (just follow the directions in the White Bread recipe instructions, page 48), and it makes fantastic sticky buns and other recipes further into the book.

Makes one 3-pound loaf, plus more for rolls or other breads. The recipe is easily doubled or halved.

INGREDIENT	VOLUME (U.S.)	WEIGHT (U.S.)	WEIGHT (METRIC)
Milk (100°F or less)	2¾ cups	I pound, 6 ounces	625 grams
Granulated yeast[1]	I tablespoon	0.35 ounce	10 grams
Kosher salt[1]	I tablespoon	0.6 ounce	17 grams
Sugar	¼ cup	2 ounces	55 grams
Unsalted butter, melted and slightly cooled	4 tablespoons (½ stick)	2 ounces	55 grams
All-purpose flour	6 cups	I pound, 14 ounces	850 grams
Egg yolk wash (I egg yolk beaten with I tablespoon water), for brushing the loaf			

[1]Can decrease to taste (see page 33).

1. Mixing and storing the dough: Add the yeast, salt, sugar, and melted butter to the milk in a 6-quart bowl or a lidded (not airtight) food container or food-grade plastic bucket.

2. Mix in the flour without kneading, using a spoon or a heavy-duty stand mixer (with paddle). If you're not using a machine, you may need to use wet hands to incorporate the last bit of flour.

3. Cover (not airtight), allow to rest at room temperature for 2 hours, and then refrigerate.

4. The dough can be used immediately after the initial rise, though it is easier to handle when cold. Refrigerate the container and use over the next 7 days or freeze. To freeze dough, see page 42.

5. On baking day, grease a 9 × 4 × 4-inch nonstick pullman loaf pan (which is taller than a standard loaf pan). Dust the surface of the refrigerated dough with flour and cut off a 3-pound (BIG cantaloupe-size) piece. Divide the dough into 3 equal pieces. Dust the pieces with more flour and quickly shape each into a ball by stretching the surface of the dough around to the bottom, rotating the ball a quarter-turn as you go.

6. Drop the 3 dough balls into the prepared pan, in a row.

7. Do not use Pullman lid, just cover loosely with plastic wrap and allow to rest at room temperature for 2 hours.

8. Preheat the oven to 350°F, with a rack placed in the center of the oven.

9. Brush the top surface with egg-yolk wash. Bake for about 50 minutes, or until caramel brown. Remove the loaf from the pan and bake for an additional 10 minutes on a baking sheet, to set the sides.

10. Allow to cool completely before serving.

Brioche

Brioche originated in the Middle Ages in Normandy, a region of France long famed for its delicious butter. Don't be alarmed at the amount of butter in the recipe; brioche is supposed to be rich and indulgent, a great addition at brunches and holiday dinners or just as sandwich bread. The name "brioche" comes from the French word *broyer*, meaning to crush or grind, due to the excessive kneading that the traditional dough required, which can be as much as 45 minutes in some recipes. Of course, with our version, we keep it to a few seconds, or you can skip the kneading altogether and have a warm loaf of brioche ready in no time flat.

Makes enough dough for at least three 1½-pound loaves. The recipe is easily doubled or halved.

INGREDIENT	VOLUME (U.S.)	WEIGHT (U.S.)	WEIGHT (METRIC)
Lukewarm water (100°F or below)	1½ cups	12 ounces	340 grams
Granulated yeast[1]	1 tablespoon	0.35 ounce	10 grams
Kosher salt[1]	1 tablespoon	0.6 ounce	17 grams
Large eggs, lightly beaten	6	12 ounces	340 grams
Honey	½ cup	6 ounces	170 grams
Unsalted butter, melted, plus butter for greasing the pan	1½ cups (3 sticks)	12 ounces	340 grams
All-purpose flour	7 cups	2 pounds, 3 ounces	990 grams
Egg wash (1 egg beaten with 1 tablespoon water), for brushing the loaf			

[1]Can decrease (see pages 15 and 33).

Visit BreadIn5.com, where you'll find recipes, photos, videos, and instructional material.

65

1. Mixing and storing the dough: Mix the water, yeast, salt, eggs, honey, and melted butter in a 6-quart bowl or a lidded (not airtight) food container.

2. Mix in the flour without kneading, using a Danish dough whisk, a spoon, or a heavy-duty stand mixer (with paddle). If you're not using a machine, you may need to use wet hands to incorporate the last bit of flour. The dough will be loose but will firm up when chilled; don't try to work with it before chilling.

3. Cover (not airtight), allow to rest at room temperature for 2 hours, and then refrigerate.

4. The dough can be used as soon as it's thoroughly chilled, at least 3 hours. Refrigerate the container and use over the next 5 days. To freeze dough, see page 42.

5. On baking day, grease an 8½ × 4½-inch nonstick loaf pan generously with butter. Dust the surface of the refrigerated dough with flour and cut off a 1½-pound (small cantaloupe–size) piece. Dust the piece with more flour and quickly shape it into a ball by stretching the surface of the dough around to the bottom, rotating the ball a quarter-turn as you go.

6. Place in the prepared pan. Cover loosely with plastic wrap and allow to rest at room temperature for 90 minutes.

DARE WE SUGGEST KNEADING? Yes, we said the dreaded "K" word. Because brioche and other enriched doughs are intended to have a tighter crumb than regular breads, a little kneading won't harm things. To get a bit more stretch in this dough, you can knead for as little as 30 seconds to really improve the texture. Just take your ball of dough and fold it over on itself several times on a floured surface, using the heel of your hand. The dough may need to rest for 10 minutes if rolling is required.

7. Preheat the oven to 350°F, with a rack placed in the center of the oven.

8. Brush the top of the loaf with egg wash.

9. Bake for about 45 minutes, or until medium golden brown and well set.

10. Allow to cool on a rack before serving.

VARIATION: BRIOCHE À TÊTE

Follow the Brioche recipe, but use 1 pound (grapefruit-size portion) of dough. Pinch off a piece the size of a ping-pong ball. Form the 2 pieces into balls. Place the larger ball in a well-buttered 8-inch fluted brioche pan. Poke a fairly deep indentation in the top of the ball of dough. This is where you will attach the tête ("head"). Form the smaller ball into a teardrop shape by tapering 1 end. Place the teardrop, pointed side down, into the indentation of the dough in the pan. Rest for 75 minutes, brush with egg wash, and bake for about 35 minutes.

Whole Wheat Brioche

This is a healthy variation on our ultradecadent brioche (page 65) that uses a balance of white and whole wheat flours. We've also reduced the amount of butter without losing the flavor. This recipe proves that you can celebrate special occasions without having to sacrifice a healthy diet. This loaf is a delicious way to sneak whole grains into kids' diets as well, as they are sure to gobble it up.

Because whole grains and butter can make this loaf a bit dense, we've added vital wheat gluten to maintain the stretch, strength, and structure of the dough. For those who aren't familiar with it, you can find it in the baking section of most grocery stores and read more in our Ingredients chapter on page 10.

Makes enough dough for at least two 2-pound loaves. The recipe is easily doubled or halved.

INGREDIENT	VOLUME (U.S.)	WEIGHT (U.S.)	WEIGHT (METRIC)
Whole wheat flour	4 cups	I pound, 2 ounces	515 grams
All-purpose flour	3 cups	15 ounces	425 grams
Granulated yeast[1]	I tablespoon	0.35 ounces	10 grams
Kosher salt[1]	I tablespoon	0.6 ounce	17 grams
Vital wheat gluten[2]	¼ cup	1½ ounces	40 grams
Lukewarm water (100°F or below)	2¼ cups	I pound, 2 ounces	510 grams
Unsalted butter, melted, plus butter for greasing the pan	12 tablespoons (1½ sticks)	6 ounces	170 grams
Large eggs, lightly beaten	5	10 ounces	285 grams
Honey	¾ cup	9 ounces	255 grams
Egg wash (I egg beaten with I tablespoon water), for brushing the loaf			

[1]Can decrease (see pages 15 and 33).
[2]See page 10

1. Mixing and storing the dough: Whisk together the flours, yeast, salt, and vital wheat gluten in a 5-quart bowl or a lidded (not airtight) food container.

2. Combine the liquid ingredients and mix them with the dry ingredients without kneading, using a heavy-duty stand mixer (with paddle), Danish dough whisk, or a spoon. You might need to use wet hands to get the last bit of flour to incorporate if you're not using a machine.

3. The dough will be loose, but it will firm up when chilled. Don't try to use it without chilling for at least 3 hours.

4. Cover (not airtight), allow to rest at room temperature for 2 hours, and then refrigerate.

5. The dough can be used as soon as it's thoroughly chilled, at least 3 hours. Refrigerate the container and use over the next 5 days. To freeze dough, see page 42.

6. On baking day, grease a brioche pan or an 8½ × 4½-inch nonstick loaf pan generously with butter. Dust the surface of the refrigerated dough with flour and cut off a 2-pound (cantaloupe-size) piece of dough. Dust the piece with more flour and quickly shape it into a ball. Place the ball in the prepared pan, cover loosely with plastic wrap and allow to rest at room temperature for 1 hour 45 minutes.

7. Preheat the oven to 350°F, with a rack placed in the center of the oven.

8. Just before baking, use a pastry brush to brush the loaf's top crust with egg wash.

9. Bake the loaf for about 50 minutes. Smaller or larger loaves will require adjustments in resting and baking time.

10. Remove the brioche from the pan (see page 36) and allow it to cool on a rack before serving.

Pumpkin Pie Bread

Autumn is the start of what we Minnesotans call the baking season, when the leaves start to change, the air is crisp, and all we want to do is pour a cup of tea as the kitchen fills up with the smell of baking bread. Pumpkin is one of the most classic fall flavors and is really the heart of the holiday meals to come. This bread is one of our favorite ways to showcase pumpkin: the orange gourd's subtle flavor blends beautifully with warm spices and is marvelous all on its own, swirled with Nutella (page 73) or cinnamon, and topped with cream cheese icing.

Makes enough dough for at least two 2-pound loaves. The recipe is easily doubled or halved.

INGREDIENT	VOLUME (U.S.)	WEIGHT (U.S.)	WEIGHT (METRIC)
All-purpose flour	7 cups	2 pounds, 3 ounces	990 grams
Granulated yeast[1]	I tablespoon	0.35 ounces	10 grams
Kosher salt[1]	I tablespoon	0.6 ounce	17 grams
Pumpkin pie spice[2]	I½ tablespoons		
Lukewarm water (100°F or below)	I cup	8 ounces	195 grams
Honey	½ cup	6 ounces	170 grams
Vegetable oil	½ cup	3½ ounces	98 grams
Pure vanilla extract	I teaspoon		
Canned pumpkin puree or a "pie" pumpkin for roasting	I¾ cups	15 ounces	425 grams
Egg yolk wash (I yolk beaten with I tablespoon water), for brushing the loaf			

[1] Can decrease (see pages I5 and 33).
[2] Or mix together 2 teaspoons ground cinnamon, I teaspoon ground ginger, ½ teaspoon freshly grated nutmeg, and ¼ teaspoon ground allspice.

PICKING PUMPKINS There are pumpkins for carving into jack-o'-lanterns and there are pumpkins for eating; the two are not interchangeable. The giant pumpkins we decorate at Halloween are fibrous, watery, flavorless, and generally trash to eat, beyond scooping out the seeds to roast. "Pie" or "sugar" pumpkins are tiny in comparison, and the flesh is tighter and dense with flavor. You can find these small baking pumpkins at the grocery store or your favorite pumpkin patch.

1. If making your own fresh pumpkin puree: Preheat the oven to 350°F. Split the "pie" pumpkin in half (see sidebar above), starting at the stem, and place it cut-side down on a baking sheet lined with foil or a silicone mat. Bake for 45 minutes. The pumpkin should be very soft all the way through when poked with a knife. Allow to cool slightly before scooping out the seeds.

2. Scoop out the roasted flesh of the pumpkin and puree it in the food processor. Set aside 1¾ cups (15 ounces) for the dough and use any leftover in your favorite pumpkin pie recipe.

3. Mixing and storing the dough: Whisk together the flour, yeast, salt, and spices in a 5-quart bowl or a lidded (not airtight) food container.

4. Combine the liquid ingredients with the pumpkin puree and mix them with the dry ingredients without kneading, using a heavy-duty stand mixer (with paddle), Danish dough whisk, or spoon. You might need to use wet hands to get the last bit of flour to incorporate if you're not using a machine.

5. The dough will be loose, but it will firm up when chilled. Don't try to use it without chilling for at least 3 hours.

6. Cover (not airtight), allow to rest at room temperature for 2 hours, and then refrigerate.

7. The dough can be used as soon as it's thoroughly chilled, at least 3 hours. Refrigerate the container and use over the next 5 days. To freeze dough, see page 42.

8. On baking day, grease a brioche pan or an 8½ x 4½-inch nonstick loaf pan. Dust the surface of the refrigerated dough with flour and cut off a 2-pound (cantaloupe-size) piece of dough. Dust the piece with more flour and quickly shape it into a ball. Place the ball in the prepared pan, cover loosely with plastic wrap, and allow to rest at room temperature for 2 hours.

9. Preheat the oven to 350°F, with a rack placed in the center of the oven.

10. Just before baking, brush the loaf's top with egg yolk wash.

11. Bake for about 50 minutes. The loaf is done when it is caramel brown and firm. Smaller or larger loaves will require adjustments in resting and baking time.

12. Remove the bread from the pan and allow it to cool on a rack before slicing and eating.

VARIATION:
NUTELLA SWIRL BREAD

1 pound Pumpkin Pie Bread dough, or any other
  enriched dough in the book
¾ cup Nutella

Follow the directions for Lemon Curd Twist (page 175), but substitute the Nutella for the lemon curd and streusel.

Buttermilk Bread

This makes a hearty loaf, a little denser than some of the other loaves, but that's exactly what we love about it.

Makes two loaves, slightly less than 2 pounds each. The recipe is easily doubled or halved.

INGREDIENT	VOLUME (U.S.)	WEIGHT (U.S.)	WEIGHT (METRIC)
Lukewarm water (100°F or below)	2 cups	16 ounces	455 grams
Buttermilk	1 cup	8½ ounces	240 grams
Granulated yeast[1]	1 tablespoon	0.35 ounce	10 grams
Kosher salt[1]	1 tablespoon	0.6 ounce	17 grams
Sugar	¼ cup	2 ounces	55 grams
All-purpose flour	6½ cups	2 pounds	910 grams
Unsalted butter, for greasing the pan and brushing the loaf			

[1]Can decrease (see pages 15 and 33).

1. Mixing and storing the dough: Mix the water, buttermilk, yeast, salt, and sugar in a 6-quart bowl or a lidded (not airtight) food container.

2. Mix in the flour without kneading, using a heavy-duty stand mixer (with paddle), a Danish dough whisk, or a spoon. If you're not using a machine, you may need to use wet hands to incorporate the last bit of flour.

3. Cover (not airtight), allow to rest at room temperature for 2 hours, and then refrigerate.

4. The dough can be used as soon as it's thoroughly chilled, at least 3 hours. Refrigerate the container and use over the next 5 days. To freeze dough, see page 42.

5. On baking day, lightly grease an 8½ × 4½-inch nonstick loaf pan. Dust the surface of the refrigerated dough with flour and cut off a 2-pound (cantaloupe-size) piece. Dust the piece with more flour and quickly shape it into a ball by stretching the surface of the dough around to the bottom, rotating the ball a quarter-turn as you go. Elongate the ball into an oval.

6. Drop the dough into the prepared pan.

7. Cover loosely with plastic wrap and allow to rest at room temperature for 90 minutes.

8. Preheat the oven to 350°F, with a rack placed in the center of the oven.

9. Brush the top surface with melted butter. Bake for about 50 minutes, or until golden brown.

10. Remove from the pan. Allow to cool completely before slicing.

Light Whole Wheat Bread

You'll find this recipe to be a basic workhorse when you want a versatile and healthy light wheat bread for sandwiches, appetizers, and snacks. The blend of all-purpose and whole wheat flours creates a bread lighter in texture, taste, and appearance than our other whole grain breads.

Makes two 2-pound loaves. The recipe is easily doubled or halved.

INGREDIENT	VOLUME (U.S.)	WEIGHT (U.S.)	WEIGHT (METRIC)
Lukewarm water (100°F or below)	3 cups	I pound, 8 ounces	680 grams
Granulated yeast[1]	I tablespoon	0.35 ounce	10 grams
Kosher salt[1]	I tablespoon	0.6 ounce	17 grams
Whole wheat flour[2]	I cup	4½ ounces	130 grams
Unbleached all-purpose flour	5½ cups	I pound, 11½ ounces	780 grams

[1]Can decrease (see pages 15 and 33).

[2]Can substitute white whole wheat flour (see page 9).

1. Mixing and storing the dough: Mix the yeast and salt with the water in a 6-quart bowl or a lidded (not airtight) food container.

2. Mix in the flours without kneading using a heavy-duty stand mixer (with paddle), a Danish dough whisk, or a spoon. If you're not using a machine, you may need to use wet hands to incorporate the last bit of flour.

3. Cover (not airtight), allow to rest at room temperature for 2 hours, and then refrigerate.

4. The dough can be used immediately after the initial rise, though it is easier to handle when cold. Refrigerate the container and use over the next 14 days. To freeze dough, see page 42.

5. On baking day, lightly grease an 8½ × 4½-inch nonstick loaf pan. Dust the surface of the refrigerated dough with flour and cut off a 2-pound (cantaloupe-size) piece. Dust the piece with more flour and quickly shape it into a ball by stretching the surface of the dough around to the bottom, rotating the ball a quarter-turn as you go. Elongate the ball into an oval.

6. Drop the loaf into the prepared pan.

7. Cover loosely with plastic wrap and allow to rest at room temperature for 90 minutes.

8. Preheat the oven to 375°F, with a rack placed in the center of the oven.

9. Lightly flour the top of the loaf and slash, using the tip of a serrated bread knife or lame. Bake for 50 to 60 minutes, or until deeply browned and firm.

10. Remove from pan and allow to cool completely before slicing.

100% Whole Wheat Bread

Whole wheat flour has a nutty, slightly bitter flavor, and it caramelizes very easily, yielding a richly browned and flavorful loaf. We've used milk and honey as tenderizers, but the honey's sweetness also serves as a nice counterpoint to whole wheat's bitter notes. Although we've showcased a Pullman pan method here, this dough also makes lovely free-form loaves using the baking stone (see page 90). If you want a lighter result in 100 percent whole-grain breads, see our *New Healthy Bread in Five Minutes a Day* (2016), where we use vital wheat gluten to get airier results with very high levels of whole grain.

Makes about four pounds of dough. The recipe is easily doubled or halved.

INGREDIENT	VOLUME (U.S.)	WEIGHT (U.S.)	WEIGHT (METRIC)
Lukewarm water (100°F or below)	1½ cups	12 ounces	340 grams
Lukewarm milk (100°F or below)	1½ cups	12 ounces	340 grams
Granulated yeast[1]	1 tablespoon	0.35 ounce	10 grams
Kosher salt[1]	1 tablespoon	0.6 ounce	17 grams
Honey	½ cup	6 ounces	170 grams
Oil	2 tablespoons	1 ounce	28 grams
Whole wheat flour[2]	7 cups	2 pounds	910 grams

[1]Can decrease (see pages 15 and 33).
[2]Can substitute white whole wheat flour (see page 9).

1. Mixing and storing the dough: Mix the water, milk, yeast, salt, honey, and oil in a 6-quart bowl or a lidded (not airtight) food container.

2. Mix in the flour without kneading, using a heavy-duty stand mixer (with paddle), a Danish dough whisk, or a spoon. If you're not using a machine, you may need to use wet hands to incorporate the last bit of flour.

3. Cover (not airtight) and allow to rest at room temperature until the dough rises, approximately 2 hours.

4. The dough can be used immediately after the initial rise, though it is easier to handle when cold. Refrigerate the container and use over the next 5 days. To freeze dough, see page 42.

5. On baking day, grease a 9 x 4 x 4-inch nonstick pullman loaf pan with butter. Dust the surface of the refrigerated dough with flour and cut off a 2½-pound (large cantaloupe-size) piece. Dust with more flour and quickly shape it into a ball by stretching the surface of the dough around to the bottom, rotating the ball a quarter-turn as you go.

6. Elongate the ball into an oval and drop it into the prepared pan. You want to fill the pan about three-quarters full, and then cover the pan with the lid.

7. Allow the dough to rest at room temperature for 1 hour and 45 minutes.

8. Preheat the oven to 350°F, with a rack placed in the center of the oven.

9. Bake for about 55 minutes, remove the lid, and bake for an additional 10 minutes. If it pops up when you remove the lid, quickly replace it and continue to bake with the lid until it is completely set.

10. Remove the loaf from the pan and allow to cool completely on a rack before slicing—otherwise you won't get well-cut sandwich slices.

Amish-Style Milk Bread

Adding an extra starch like potato flour gives bread a lift and lightness that you'd not expect from a lowly spud. This dough is one of our favorites for its rising power and flavor. Divided into small pieces and layered with lots of butter, it is the base for our springy but rich Parker House Rolls (page 113) or it makes a gorgeous Raspberry Braid (page 312). After you make this dough, cruise through the book and find a world of possibilities.

Makes two 2-pound loaves. The recipe is easily doubled or halved.

INGREDIENT	VOLUME (U.S.)	WEIGHT (U.S.)	WEIGHT (METRIC)
Whole milk	2½ cups	1 pound, 4 ounces	565 grams
Large eggs	2	4 ounces	115 grams
Granulated yeast[1]	1 tablespoon	0.35 ounce	10 grams
Kosher salt[1]	1 tablespoon	0.6 ounce	17 grams
Sugar	⅓ cup	2¼ ounces	65 grams
All-purpose flour	6¼ cups	1 pounds, 15 ounces	885 grams
Potato flour	¼ cup	1¾ ounces	50 grams
Unsalted butter, melted and slightly cooled	8 tablespoons (1 stick)	4 ounces	115 grams
Egg wash (1 egg beaten with 1 tablespoon water), for brushing the loaf			

[1]Can decrease (see pages 15 and 33).

1. Mixing and storing the dough: Mix the milk, eggs, yeast, salt, and sugar in a 6-quart bowl or a lidded (not airtight) food container.

2. Mix the flours and butter with the milk mixture without kneading, using a heavy-duty stand mixer (with paddle), a Danish dough whisk, or a spoon.

3. Cover (not airtight), allow to rest at room temperature for 2 hours, and then refrigerate.

4. The dough can be used as soon as it's thoroughly chilled, at least 3 hours. Refrigerate the container and use over the next 5 days. To freeze dough, see page 42.

5. On baking day, grease an 8½ x 4½-inch nonstick loaf pan. Dust the surface of the refrigerated dough with flour and cut off a 2-pound (large cantaloupe-size) piece. Dust with more flour and quickly shape it into a ball by stretching the surface of the dough around to the bottom, rotating the ball a quarter-turn as you go. Elongate the ball into an oval and place it in the loaf pan.

6. Cover loosely with plastic wrap and allow to rest at room temperature for 90 minutes.

7. Preheat the oven to 350°F, with a rack placed in the center of the oven.

8. Brush the top crust with egg wash.

9. Bake for about 50 minutes, or until the loaf is browned and firm.

10. Remove from the pan and allow to cool on a rack before serving.

Chocolate Bread

Makes two 2-pound loaves. The recipe is easily doubled or halved.

INGREDIENT	VOLUME (U.S.)	WEIGHT (U.S.)	WEIGHT (METRIC)
Lukewarm water (100°F or below)	2½ cups	1 pound, 4 ounces	565 grams
Vegetable oil	½ cup	3½ ounces	100 grams
Granulated yeast[1]	1 tablespoon	0.35 ounces	10 grams
Kosher salt[1]	1 tablespoon	0.6 ounce	17 grams
Sugar	1 cup	7 ounces	200 grams
All-purpose flour	6 cups	1 pound, 4 ounces	850 grams
Unsweetened cocoa powder, preferably dark	¾ cup	3 ounces	85 grams
Bittersweet chocolate, chopped fine	1 cup	4 ounces	115 grams
Egg white wash (1 egg white beaten with 1 tablespoon water), for brushing the loaf.			

[1]Can decrease (see pages 15 and 33).

1. Mixing and storing the dough: Mix the water, oil, yeast, salt, and sugar in a 6-quart bowl or a lidded (not airtight) food container.

2. Mix in the flour, cocoa powder, and chopped chocolate without kneading, using a heavy-duty stand mixer (with paddle), a Danish dough whisk, or a spoon. If you're not using a machine, you may need to use wet hands to incorporate the last bit of flour.

3. Cover (not airtight) and allow to rest at room temperature until the dough rises for 2 hours.

Visit BreadIn5.com, where you'll find recipes, photos, videos, and instructional material.

85

4. The dough can be used immediately after the initial rise, though it is easier to handle when cold. Refrigerate the container and use over the next 5 days. To freeze dough, see page 42.

5. On baking day, lightly grease an 8½ × 4½-inch nonstick loaf pan. Dust the surface of the refrigerated dough with flour and cut off a 2-pound (cantaloupe-size) piece. Dust the piece with more flour and quickly shape it into a ball by stretching the surface of the dough around to the bottom, rotating the ball a quarter-turn as you go. Elongate the ball into an oval. Drop the dough into the prepared pan.

6. Cover loosely with plastic wrap and allow to rest at room temperature for 90 minutes.

7. Preheat the oven to 350°F, with a rack placed in the center of the oven.

8. Brush the top surface with egg wash. Bake for about 50 minutes, or until set firm when you gently press on the top of the loaf. You can't judge doneness by color on this one.

9. Remove from the pan and allow to cool completely before serving.

7

SMALL LOAVES, ROLLS, AND BUNS

Semolina Bread

Semolina has a beautiful yellow color and wonderfully mellow, winey-sweet flavor. We love those aspects of bread made with durum flour, but used on its own, the hard nature of this flour would produce a very dense bread, so we always mix it with bread flour. This dough is the perfect base for Istanbul Simit (page 93), a variety of pitas (pages 121–127), or even Hamburger Buns (page 106).

Makes 4 loaves, slightly less than 1 pound each. The recipe is easily doubled or halved.

INGREDIENT	VOLUME (U.S.)	WEIGHT (U.S.)	WEIGHT (METRIC)
Lukewarm water (100°F or below)	2¾ cups	1 pound, 6 ounces	625 grams
Olive oil	¼ cup	2 ounces	55 grams
Granulated yeast[1]	1 tablespoon	0.35 ounce	10 grams

(Continued)			
Kosher salt[1]	I tablespoon	0.6 ounce	17 grams
Durum (semolina) flour	I cup	5½ ounces	155 grams
Bread flour	6 cups	I pound, 14 ounces	850 grams
Sesame seeds for top of bread	2 tablespoons		

[1]Can decrease (see pages 15 and 33).

1. Mixing and storing the dough: Mix the water, oil, yeast, and salt in a 6-quart bowl, or a lidded (not airtight) food container.

2. Mix in the flours without kneading, using a heavy-duty stand mixer (with paddle), a Danish dough whisk, or a spoon. If you're not using a machine, you may need to use wet hands to incorporate the last bit of flour.

3. Cover (not airtight) and allow to rest at room temperature until the dough rises for 2 hours.

4. The dough can be used immediately after the initial rise, though it is easier to handle when cold. Refrigerate the container and use over the next 14 days.

5. On baking day, prepare a pizza peel with cornmeal or parchment paper. Dust the surface of the refrigerated dough with flour and cut off a 1-pound (grapefruit-size) piece. Dust the piece with more flour and quickly shape it into a ball by stretching the surface of the dough around to the bottom, rotating the ball a quarter-turn as you go. Elongate the ball to form an oval-shaped free-form loaf. Cover loosely with plastic wrap and allow to rest at room temperature for 60 minutes (see sidebar, White Bread Master Recipe, step 6, page 52).

6. Preheat a baking stone near the middle of the oven to 450°F, with an empty metal broiler tray on any shelf that won't interfere with rising bread.

7. Brush the surface with water, sprinkle with sesame seeds, and slash the surface with ½-inch-deep parallel cuts, using a serrated bread knife.

8. Slide the loaf directly onto the hot stone. Pour 1 cup of hot tap water into the broiler tray and quickly close the oven door (see page 29 for steam alternatives). Bake for 30 to 35 minutes, or until deeply browned and firm. Smaller or larger loaves will require adjustments in resting and baking time.

9. Allow to cool on a rack before serving.

Visit BreadIn5.com, where you'll find recipes, photos, videos, and instructional material.

91

Simit

Simit is a ubiquitous Istanbul street food, carried stacked high on the heads of vendors. When Zoë and her family visited the city, these twisted rings of dough, encrusted with sesame seeds and baked golden brown, were a daily snack—both because they are delicious and because the sellers were such a spectacle, outdoing each other with height and balance. Simit might appear similar to bagels, but they are not boiled, and they include the distinctive flavor of *pekmez,* a fruit-based syrup not unlike molasses. It can be found at Middle Eastern and Turkish grocery stores and online, or replaced with molasses.

Makes 8 simit

All-purpose flour, for dusting

1 ½ pounds (small cantaloupe–size portion) Semolina Bread dough (page 89), Light Whole Wheat dough (page 77), or White Bread Master Recipe dough (page 48)

½ cup pekmez syrup or molasses

1 cup water

1 cup sesame seeds, for dredging

1. To bake: Line a baking sheet with parchment paper or a silicone mat. Dust the surface of the refrigerated dough with flour and cut off a 1½-pound (small cantaloupe–size) piece. Divide the dough into 8 equal pieces. Dust each piece with more flour and quickly shape it into a ball by stretching the surface of the dough around to the bottom, rotating the ball a quarter-turn as you go. Cover loosely with plastic wrap and allow to rest at room temperature for 30 minutes.

2. Mix the pekmez and the water in a bowl.

3. Place the sesame seeds in a dry skillet and heat over medium heat until toasted.

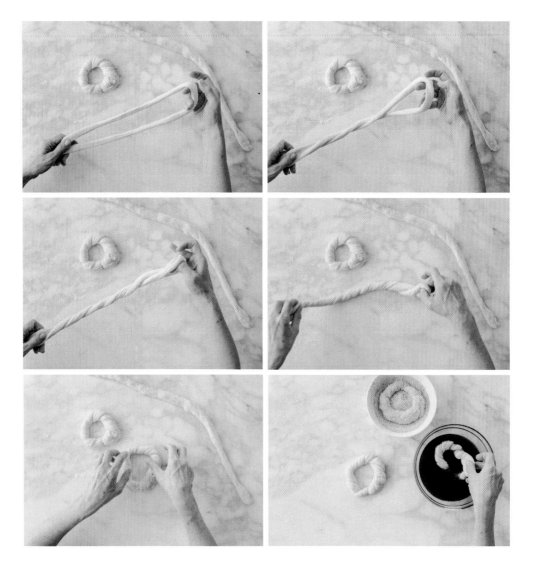

4. Elongate each ball, dusting with additional flour as necessary. Roll it back and forth with your hands on a flour-dusted surface to form a ½-inch-thick rope about 20 inches long. If the dough springs back and won't stretch easily, leave it to sit for 5 minutes and try again.

5. Fold one of the ropes in half and wind it into a tightly twisted rope. Join the ends to form a circle. Roll the joined ends together to make sure they are secure. Dip the simit in the diluted pekmez and then dredge both sides in the sesame seeds. Place the simit on the prepared baking sheet. Repeat with the remaining ropes.

6. Preheat a baking stone near the middle of the oven to 450°F, with an empty metal broiler tray on any shelf that won't interfere with rising simit.

7. Allow to rest at room temperature for 20 to 30 minutes.

8. Place the baking sheet directly on the hot baking stone. Pour 1 cup of hot tap water into the broiler tray and quickly close the oven door (see page 29 for steam alternatives). Bake for about 25 minutes, or until golden brown and firm.

9. These can be served hot from the oven.

Bagels

These bagels are similar in taste, texture, and appearance to Montreal bagels, which are made with honey, encrusted with seeds, and baked in a wood-fired oven. We deliver on the honey, but we bake them in our regular electric ovens, and they are still wonderful.

Makes 6 bagels

I pound (grapefruit-size portion) Super Strong Dough (page 59)
    or any other non-enriched dough in the book
All-purpose flour, for dusting
I cup sesame or poppy seeds, for topping the bagels

FOR THE BOILING POT
8 quarts water
¼ cup malt powder or honey
I teaspoon baking soda

1. To boil and bake, preheat a baking stone near the middle of the oven to 500°F, with an empty metal broiler tray on any shelf that won't interfere with the bagels.

2. Dust the surface of the refrigerated dough with flour and cut off a 1-pound (grapefruit-size) piece. Divide the dough into 6 equal pieces. Dust each piece with more flour and quickly shape it into a 12-inch-long rope by stretching the dough and rolling it between your palms and the surface. (If the ropes won't stretch that long, just let them sit for several minutes and they will stretch more easily.) Pinch together the 2 ends to form a circle.

3. Cover them loosely with plastic wrap and allow to rest at room temperature for about 20 minutes.

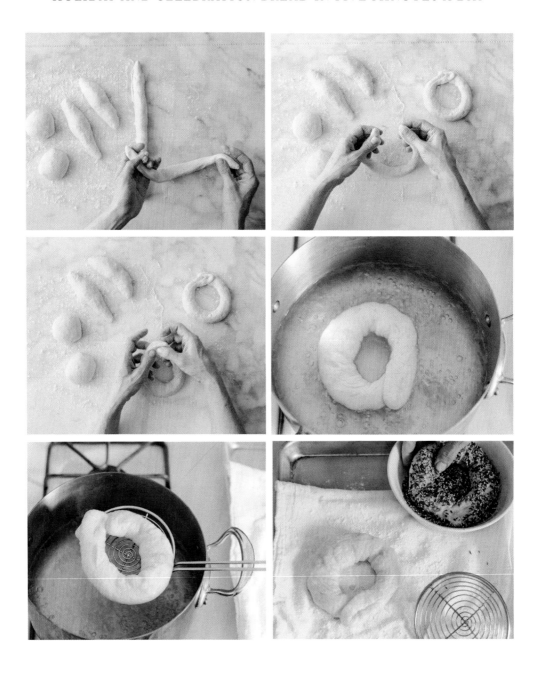

4. Prepare the boiling pot: Bring the water to a boil. Reduce to a simmer and add the malt powder and baking soda. Dust a clean kitchen towel with flour.

5. Ease the hole of each bagel open until its diameter is about triple the width of the bagel wall.

6. Drop the bagels into the simmering water one at a time, raising the heat as necessary to continue at a slow simmer. Let them simmer for 1 minute and then flip them over with a slotted spoon to cook the other side for another 30 seconds.

7. Remove the bagels from the water using the slotted spoon, and place on the prepared kitchen towel. This will absorb some of the excess water. After they've drained a bit, dredge them in the seeds. Place them on a pizza peel.

8. Slide the bagels directly onto the hot stone. Pour 1 cup of hot tap water into the broiler tray, and quickly close the oven door (see page 29 for steam alternatives). Bake for about 20 minutes, or until deeply browned and firm.

9. Break the usual rule for cooling and serve these a bit warm—they're fantastic!

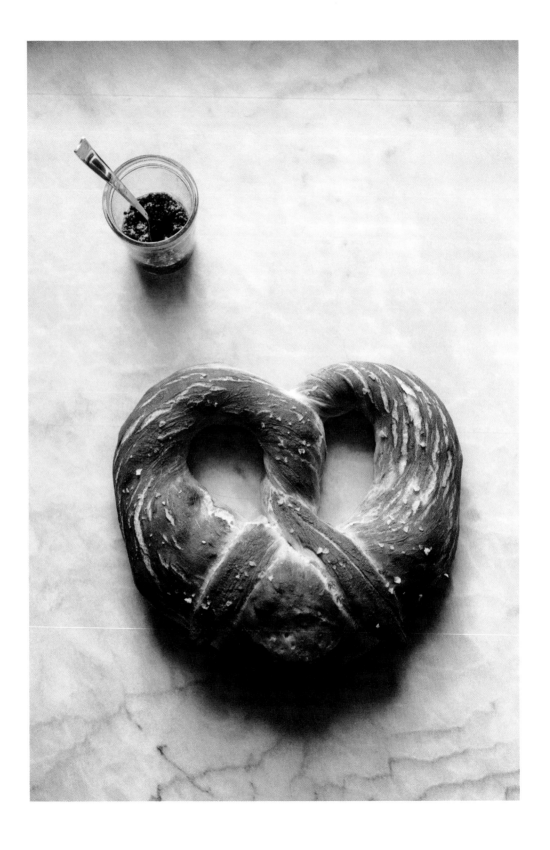

Family-Size Soft Pretzel

This pretzel is a showpiece and meant to be shared. Its giant size gives a perfect ratio of salty crust to the soft crumb within. Because it's so ginormous, we skip the traditional boiling and just brush on the baking soda wash to get the flavor and color we love. Both Jeff and Zoë grew up near New York City and ate soft pretzels with nothing more than yellow mustard, but now they prefer a mustard with a little more bite. The style of mustard is up to you, but a stein of beer is recommended.

Makes 1 giant pretzel

1 pound (grapefruit-size portion)
    Super Strong Dough (page 59)
All-purpose flour, for dusting
Coarse sea salt or "pretzel" salt, for
    topping the pretzel

SODA WASH

½ cup water

1 tablespoon baking soda

Mustard, for serving

WE DIDN'T TRY LYE IN THE BOILING POT: When we published a pretzel recipe in our earlier books, a few people wrote to express their dismay that we didn't use lye in the boiling pot—that's right, drain cleaner. They claimed that it's the crucial ingredient to get the absolutely authentic German-style pretzel crust they craved. They may have a point, but we doubted we'd be able to convince home bakers to try this particularly wacky ingredient. We actually went so far as to purchase food-grade lye, but then we read the label: *"wear chemical-resistant gloves. Wear protective clothing. Wear goggles. . ."* And our favorite, advising users to watch out for *"digestive tract burns"* (though the manufacturer helpfully advises against swallowing the lye). We found that baking soda makes a terrific substitute—it's alkaline enough. We must admit, we never opened that container of lye.

1. To shape: Dust the surface of the refrigerated dough with flour and cut off a 1-pound (grapefruit-size) piece. Dust the piece with more flour and quickly shape it into a ball by stretching the surface of the dough around to the bottom, rotating the ball a quarter-turn as you go. Elongate the ball, dusting with additional flour as necessary. Roll it back and forth with your hands on a flour-dusted surface to form a rope about 36 inches long, approximately 4 inches in diameter at the center, and tapered very thin on the ends. If it resists stretching, let the dough rest for 5 minutes and try again.

2. Twist the dough rope into a pretzel shape by first forming a horseshoe with the ends facing away from you. Fold the tapered ends down to the thick part of the rope, crossing them one over the other. Extend the ends an inch beyond the bottom loop and gently press them together. Place the pretzel on parchment paper that has been dusted with flour. Cover loosely with plastic wrap and allow to rest at room temperature for 45 minutes.

3. Preheat a baking stone near the middle of the oven to 450°F, with an empty metal broiler tray on any shelf that won't interfere with rising pretzels.

4. Prepare the soda wash: Heat the water and baking soda in a small pan until the soda dissolves. Paint the pretzel with the soda wash and sprinkle with the salt.

5. Place the pretzel and the parchment paper directly onto the hot stone. Pour 1 cup of hot tap water into the broiler tray and quickly close the oven door (see page 29 for steam alternatives). Bake for about 25 minutes, or until deeply browned and firm.

6. Serve a bit warm, with mustard.

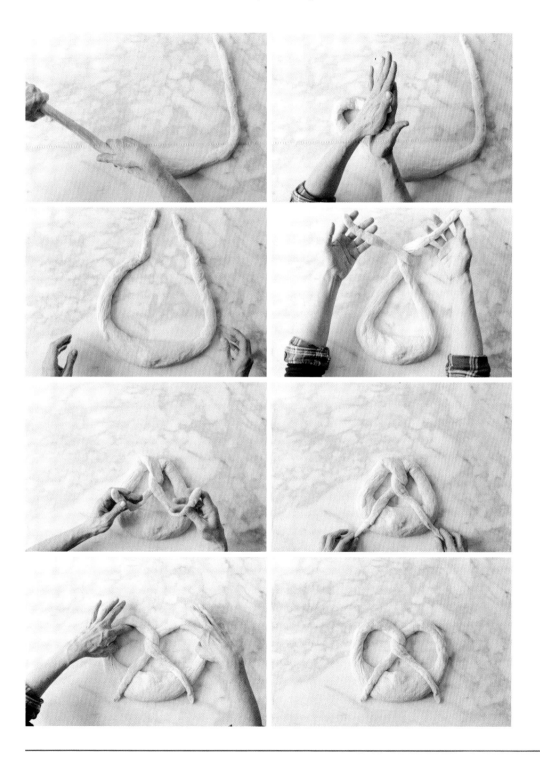

VARIATION: PRETZEL BUNS

Divide a 1-pound (grapefruit-size) piece of Super Strong Dough (page 59) into 8 pieces, form them into smooth balls, and then cover and allow to rest for 20 minutes. Space them 2 inches apart on a baking sheet lined with parchment paper or a silicone mat. Brush with the baking soda wash, slash a cross on the top of the buns with a serrated knife, sprinkle with coarse salt, and bake with steam for 20 minutes at 450°F.

Soft Dinner Rolls

Rolls are quick and easy to bake. They're small, so they need very little resting time before they go into the oven. And they don't have to cool completely like larger loaves do—it's okay to eat them slightly warm.

Makes five 3-ounce rolls

I pound (grapefruit-size portion) White Bread Master Recipe dough (page 48), Amish-Style Milk Bread dough (page 83), Challah dough (page 147), Whole Wheat Brioche dough (page 68), Semolina Bread dough (page 89), or any other dough in the book
All-purpose flour, for dusting
Melted butter, for brushing the rolls

1. To bake: Preheat the oven to 350°F, with a rack placed in the center of the oven.

2. Dust the surface of the refrigerated dough with flour and cut off a 1-pound (grapefruit-size) piece. Divide the dough into 5 equal pieces and quickly shape into balls.

3. Place them 2 inches apart on a baking sheet lined with parchment paper or a silicone mat, cover loosely with plastic wrap, and allow to rest at room temperature for 30 minutes.

4. Cut a cross into the top of each roll with a serrated knife or kitchen shears (keep the shears perpendicular to your work surface when you cut).

5. Brush the tops with melted butter and place the baking sheet in the oven. Bake for about 25 minutes, or until richly browned.

6. For the softest result, brush with more butter. Serve slightly warm.

To make soft pull-apart rolls: Cut off a 1-pound (grapefruit-size) piece of Challah dough (page 147), Brioche dough (page 65), or Buttermilk Bread dough (page 74), divide the dough into 8 pieces, and quickly shape them into balls. Place the dough balls in a greased 8 × 8-inch baking dish; they should be touching. Cover and allow to rest for 30 minutes, and then brush the tops with melted butter. Bake at 350°F for about 30 minutes, or until golden brown. Brush again with melted butter and serve slightly warm.

VARIATION: HAMBURGER BUNS

Every good celebration has burgers, so what kind of book would this be without a bun?

Follow the directions for Soft Dinner Rolls, but flatten the 5 balls to ¼-inch-thick disks. Cover and let them rest for 45 minutes. Brush the tops with butter (do not slash) and sprinkle with sesame seeds. Bake for about 25 minutes, or until golden brown and set. Allow to cool before slicing.

Sandwich "Subs"

Makes six 8-inch sandwich buns

Here in Minnesota, most people call sandwiches made on these long rolls "subways" or "subs." On the East Coast, Philadelphians eat "hoagies." Native New Yorkers might know them best as "heroes," while up in Maine people prefer the more descriptive "Italian sandwiches." Whatever you call them, no one can resist these long sandwiches. The buns have a soft interior and are made with steam in the oven to give them just a bit of a crust. You can pick just about any dough to use, but if you want a crisper crust, pick a dough that doesn't have eggs, nor a lot of fat or sugar.

> 2 pounds (cantaloupe-size portion) White Bread Master Recipe dough (page 48), Amish-Style Milk Bread dough (page 83), Challah dough (page 147), Whole Wheat dough (page 68), Semolina Bread dough (page 89), Olive Oil Dough (page 119), or any other dough in the book
>
> All-purpose flour, for dusting
>
> Egg white wash (1 egg white beaten with 1 tablespoon water), for brushing the rolls

1. Dust the surface of the refrigerated dough with flour and cut off a 2-pound (cantaloupe-size) piece. Divide the dough into 6 equal pieces. Dust each piece with more flour and quickly shape them into 10-inch logs by stretching the dough and rolling it between your palms and the surface. If they won't stretch that long, just let them sit for several minutes and they will stretch more easily.

2. Place the ropes on a baking sheet lined with parchment paper. Cover loosely with plastic wrap and allow to rest at room temperature for 45 minutes. A longer rest will result in a softer bread, so try 60 minutes if you have time.

3. Preheat the oven to 350°F, with a rack placed in the center of the oven.

4. Brush the dough with the egg white wash.

5. Place the baking sheet in the oven, pour 1 cup of hot tap water into the broiler tray, and quickly close the oven door. Bake for about 25 minutes, or until richly browned. Serve slightly warm, stuffed with your favorite sandwich fixings.

VARIATION: HOT DOG BUNS

Just make the subway rolls smaller.

Follow the recipe for Sandwich "Subs", but divide the dough into 12 equal pieces and form them into 5-inch ropes that are about 1 inch wide. Reduce the baking time to about 20 minutes.

Mallorca Buns

Mallorca buns are a treat from Puerto Rico by way of Majorca, Spain. The coiled shape of these sugar-dusted buns is inspired by the Majorcan *ensaïmada,* a savory pastry with pork. By the time this bun was incorporated into Puerto Rican culture, however, it had become a sweet, egg-enriched bun, suitable for breakfast or accompanying an afternoon *café con leche.* They are at their very best served warm from the oven and eaten slowly. The heavenly lightness and fluffiness are made to be savored. *"These became a morning pilgrimage when I was in Puerto Rico with my family. Every morning we'd walk 1½ miles to the public road, call a cab, and drive into the village to our favorite bakery. By the end of the trip, the shop owner would place a dozen in a box for us as we got out of the cab. A few would never make it past the door."* —Zoë

Makes 12 buns

> 2 pounds (cantaloupe-size portion) Brioche dough (page 65), Amish-Style Milk Bread dough (page 83), or Challah dough (page 147)
>
> All-purpose flour, for dusting
>
> Egg wash (1 egg beaten with 1 tablespoon water), for brushing the buns
>
> Confectioners' sugar, for dusting the buns

1. Dust the dough with flour and roll it out to a ¼-inch-thick rectangle, about 10 × 18 inches. Using a pastry wheel, cut 12 even strips.

2. Stretch each strip to be 12 inches long and roll the ends between your palms to taper. Coil each strip to make a spiral bun, tucking the end under the bun.

3. Place the buns on a baking sheet lined with parchment paper, making sure they have enough room to rise without touching. Cover loosely with plastic wrap and allow to rest at room temperature for 45 minutes.

4. Preheat the oven to 350°F, with a rack placed in the center of the oven.

5. Brush the tops with egg wash. Bake for about 25 minutes, or until light golden in color and firm to the touch.

6. Allow the buns to cool.

7. Sift a generous layer of confectioners' sugar over the top of buns. They're excellent with a cup of coffee.

Parker House Rolls

These folded-over rolls take their name from the historic Parker House Hotel in Boston. According to tradition, a cook at the hotel kitchen was so infuriated with a demanding guest that she threw a tray of unbaked rolls at the wall. When they emerged from the oven, they had gained their distinctive flattened shape, and they quickly became a favorite. Over the decades, the Parker House Hotel hosted many prominent members of society, including Mark Twain and Ralph Waldo Emerson. It's easy to picture these distinguished writers scrawling notes over a warm Parker House roll.

Makes 12 rolls

I pound (grapefruit-size portion) Amish-Style Milk Bread dough (page 83), Challah dough (page 147), or Brioche dough (page 65)

All-purpose flour, for dusting

4 tablespoons (½ stick) salted butter, melted, for brushing the dough

1. To bake: Butter an 8 × 8-inch square cake pan. Dust the dough with flour and quickly shape it into a ball by stretching the surface of the dough around to the bottom, rotating the ball a quarter-turn as you go.

2. Roll the dough out to a ¼-inch-thick rectangle, about 8 × 12 inches. Brush the surface of the dough with melted butter. Cut the dough down the center of the short end and then fold each of the 2 pieces in half. Divide each doubled over strip into 6 equal pieces, for a total of 12 rolls.

3. Place the rolls in the pan so they are touching. Cover loosely with plastic wrap and allow to rest at room temperature for 45 minutes.

4. Preheat the oven to 350°F, with a rack placed in the center of the oven.

5. Brush the tops of the rolls with more melted butter. Bake for 25 to 30 minutes, or until golden brown.

6. Allow to cool slightly before eating. Serve with even more butter.

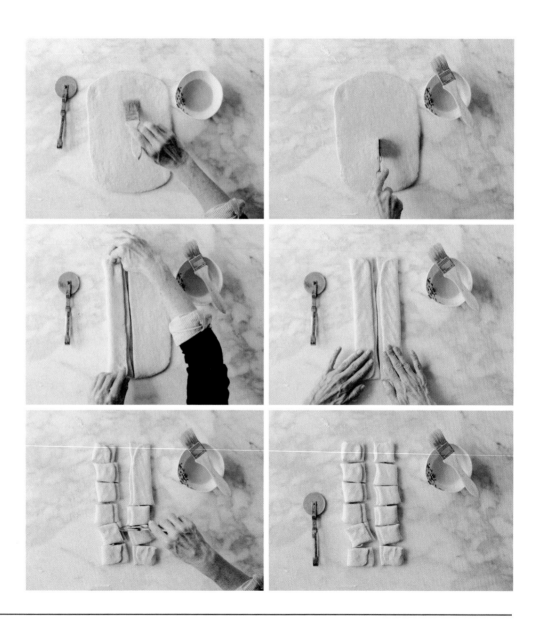

Conchas

Concha is the Spanish word for "seashell," a fitting name for these Mexican pastries. When wheat flour was introduced to the region, the indigenous people, more accustomed to corn tortillas, did not like the taste of European breads and preferred to add sugar. This cultural sweet tooth resulted in countless varieties of *pan dulce*, or sweet bread, including the concha. Today conchas can be found fresh-baked on almost any street corner in Mexico. Conchas use a traditional French-style brioche or enriched dough, but the sugar cookie–like crust is a Mexican innovation. We took that cookie concept even further and added decorating sugar. It is typical to dip conchas into sweetened coffee or hot chocolate for an afternoon snack.

Makes 12 buns

I pound (cantaloupe-size portion) Challah dough (page 147), Brioche dough (page 65), or any other enriched dough in the book

All-purpose flour, for dusting

Egg wash (1 egg beaten with 1 tablespoon water), for brushing the buns

Decorating sugar, for sprinkling on the buns

COOKIE DOUGH

4 tablespoons (½ stick) unsalted butter, at room temperature

¼ cup sugar

½ cup all-purpose flour

Pinch salt

I egg white

¼ teaspoon almond extract

¼ teaspoon ground cinnamon (optional; it will make the cookie dough brown, so don't use if using food coloring)

Food coloring (optional)

1. Dust the surface of the refrigerated dough with flour and cut off a 1-pound (grapefruit-size) piece. Dust the piece with more flour and quickly shape it into a ball by stretching the surface of the dough around to the bottom, rotating the ball a quarter-turn as you go. Divide the dough into 8 pieces and shape them into balls.

2. Place the dough balls on a baking sheet lined with parchment paper. Cover loosely with plastic wrap and allow to rest at room temperature for 60 minutes.

3. Preheat the oven to 350°F, with a rack placed in the center of the oven.

4. Prepare the cookie dough: As the dough balls are resting, mix all the ingredients in a large bowl; cover with plastic and refrigerate.

5. Once the dough balls have rested, brush the tops with the egg wash. Roll out the cookie dough and stamp out 8 rounds; you decide how big. (Traditionally, the cookie would cover the entire bun, but we like them just with a jaunty cap of cookie.) Gently brush the cookies with water, sprinkle them with decorating sugar, and place on top of the buns. (There will be leftover cookie dough to bake off as cookies or save for another batch of conchas.)

6. Bake for 25 to 30 minutes, or until the bread crust is golden brown and the cookies are still pale.

7. Allow to cool on a rack before serving.

8

FLATBREADS

Olive Oil Dough

This versatile, rich dough is terrific for these flatbreads, but also works as a great sandwich roll (page 107). The fruitier the olive oil, the better the flavor.

Makes four loaves, slightly less than 1 pound each. The recipe is easily doubled or halved.

INGREDIENT	VOLUME (U.S.)	WEIGHT (U.S.)	WEIGHT (METRIC)
Lukewarm water (100°F or below)	2¾ cups	1 pound, 6 ounces	625 grams
Granulated yeast[1]	1 tablespoon	0.35 ounce	10 grams
Kosher salt[1]	1 tablespoon	0.6 ounce	17 grams
Sugar	1 tablespoon	½ ounce	15 grams
Olive oil	¼ cup	1¾ ounces	50 grams
All-purpose flour	6½ cups	2 pounds, ½ ounce	920 grams

[1]Can decrease (see pages 15 and 33).

1. Mix the water, yeast, salt, sugar, and olive oil in a 6-quart bowl or a lidded (not airtight) food container.

2. Mix in the flour without kneading, using a heavy-duty stand mixer (with paddle), a Danish dough whisk, or a spoon. If you're not using a machine, you may need to use wet hands to incorporate the last bit of flour.

3. Cover (not airtight) and allow to rest at room temperature until the dough rises for 2 hours.

4. The dough can be used immediately after the initial rise, though it is easier to handle when cold. Refrigerate the container and use over the next 12 days. To freeze dough, see page 42.

Pita

Pita bread is the puffy, flour-dusted flatbread of the Middle East. It is a simple and elemental bread, and for reasons we can't explain at all, it's just about our most fragrant one. Aside from being delicious, this bread is among the fastest in the book to make. It's easy to produce beautiful, puffed loaves. The secret to the puffing is to roll the dough thinly and use a hot oven. Because pita isn't slashed, internal steam is trapped inside. As soon as the top and bottom crusts set, steam in the interior pushes them apart. It can't miss! Pita is delicious warm from the oven—unlike loaf breads, it doesn't need to cool completely.

Try the rich Bosphorus Pita variation that is made with Challah dough (page 147).

Makes one 8-inch pita, or 2 small individual pitas

½ pound (orange-size portion) Olive Oil Dough (page 119), Super Strong Dough (page 59), 100% Whole Wheat Bread dough (page 79), Light Whole Wheat Bread dough (page 77), or Semolina Bread dough (page 89)

All-purpose flour, for dusting

1. Preheat a baking stone to 500°F, on a rack placed in the center of the oven.

2. Dust the surface of the refrigerated dough with flour and cut off a ½-pound (orange-size) piece. Dust the piece with more flour and quickly shape it into a ball by stretching the surface of the dough around to the bottom, rotating the ball a quarter-turn as you go. Place the dough on a flour-dusted pizza peel.

3. Using your hands and a rolling pin, roll the dough out into a ⅛-inch-thick round, about 12 inches wide. This is crucial, because if it's too thick, it may not puff. You'll need to sprinkle the peel lightly with white flour as you work, occasionally flipping the dough to prevent sticking to the rolling pin or to the board. Use a dough scraper to remove the round of dough from the peel if it sticks. Do not slash the pita, or it will

not puff. No rest or rise time is needed. (If you are making individual pitas, divide the dough into two before forming.)

4. Place the tip of the peel near the back of the stone, close to where you want the far edge of the pita to land. Give the peel a few quick forward-and-back jiggles and pull it sharply out from under the dough. Bake for 6 to 8 minutes, or until lightly browned and puffed. You may need to transfer the pita to a higher shelf (without the stone) to achieve browning.

5. For the most authentic, soft-crusted pita, wrap in a clean cotton dish towel and set on a cooling rack when baking is complete. The pita will deflate slightly as it cools. The space between crusts will still be there, but may have to be nudged apart with a fork.

6. Serve the pita as sandwich pockets or tear it into pieces. If not using right away, store cooled pita in plastic bags. Unlike hard-crusted breads, pitas are not harmed by airtight storage.

VARIATION: BOSPHORUS PITA

"I had this pita in Orlando, Florida, at a restaurant called Bosphorus. The pita arrived at our table still puffed from the oven and a golden caramel color. It was like no pita I'd ever had before or since and I am thrilled to have figured out this close approximation to that exciting flatbread, which isn't flat at all."— Zoë

Makes one 12-inch pita

Follow the Pita recipe directions for the single large pita, but brush the dough with egg wash before baking.

   1 pound (grapefruit-size portion) Challah dough (page 147) or Yogurt Challah dough (page 151)

   Egg yolk wash (1 egg yolk beaten with 1 tablespoon water), for brushing the dough

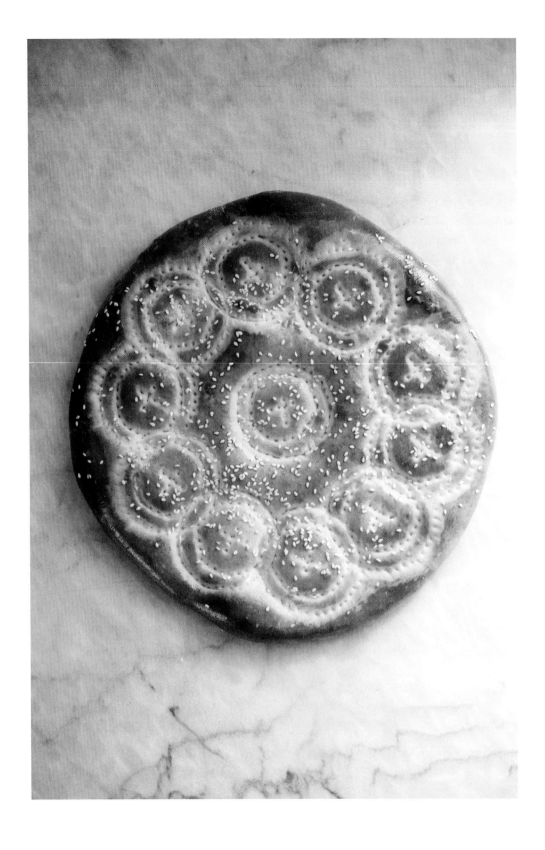

Ramadan Pita

This is loosely based on a special pita (or *pide*) served in Turkey during Ramadan. It is traditionally decorated with a crosshatch on the surface, but we went with a more ornate design. No matter how you design the top, this bread is delicious and certainly does bring together family and friends as the holiday intends. This pita is thicker and doesn't create a pocket.

Makes one 9-inch pita

> 1 pound (grapefruit-size portion) Semolina Bread dough (page 89)
>
> All-purpose flour, for dusting
>
> Egg yolk wash (1 egg yolk beaten with 1 tablespoon water), for brushing the pita
>
> Sesame seeds, for sprinkling on the pita

1. Dust the surface of the refrigerated dough with flour and cut off a 1-pound (grape-fruit-size) piece. Dust the piece with more flour and quickly shape it into a ball by stretching the surface of the dough around to the bottom, rotating the ball a quarter-turn as you go. Place the dough on a flour-dusted surface.

2. Using your hands and a rolling pin, roll the dough out into a ½-inch-thick round, about 9 inches wide. This is crucial, because if it's too thin, it may puff. Place the dough on a flour-dusted piece of parchment paper on a baking sheet. Cover loosely with plastic wrap and allow to rest at room temperature for 45 minutes.

3. Preheat a baking stone to 400°F, with a rack placed in the center of the oven.

4. While the oven preheats, use your fingertips to create a crosshatch design or use the edge of a drinking glass, dipped in flour, to create circles. You want to make an

impression in the dough, but not cut through it. Once you've created your design, go over the design with a fork. This will prevent the dough from puffing and ruining your pattern.

5. Brush very lightly with egg yolk wash and sprinkle with sesame seeds. You don't want the egg wash to get into the creases, or the design won't be as defined.

6. Bake for about 25 minutes, or until lightly browned.

7. Serve immediately. It is lovely warm from the oven.

Sheermal

This saffron and cardamom flatbread has roots in Persia and is made in Northern India, Pakistan, and Iran at the end of *Ramzan* (Ramadan). We found it fascinating how similar it is to breads made in Scandinavia using saffron and cardamom. The style of baking couldn't be more different, but the similarity of the dough shows how the influences of one country travel the world and take root.

Makes four 6-inch flatbreads

I pound (grapefruit-size portion) Saint Lucia Saffron Buns dough (page 261)

All-purpose flour, for dusting

¼ cup milk

Pinch saffron

Pinch salt

I tablespoon unsalted butter or ghee, melted (page 12)

1. Preheat a baking stone to 400°F, with a rack placed in the center of the oven.

2. Dust the surface of the refrigerated dough with flour and cut off a 1-pound (grapefruit-size) piece. Divide the dough into 4 equal pieces. Dust the pieces with more flour and quickly shape each one into a ball by stretching the surface of the dough around to the bottom, rotating the ball a quarter-turn as you go.

3. Using your hands and a rolling pin, roll 1 dough ball out into a ¼-inch-thick round about 6 inches wide. Place the dough on a baking sheet lined with parchment paper. Repeat with the remaining dough.

4. Bring the milk, saffron, and salt to a simmer in a small saucepan. Let sit until the milk is golden from the saffron.

5. Poke the dough many times with a fork to prevent the dough from puffing in the oven.

6. Brush with the saffron milk.

7. Bake for about 15 minutes, or until golden and set. Brush the flatbreads with melted butter as soon as they come out of the oven.

8. Serve immediately. The flatbread is lovely warm or cooled.

Lavash

Armenian lavash is believed to be among the world's oldest breads, dating back as many as ten thousand years. This simple flatbread makes a great vehicle to mop up sauces or to serve with soups and dips.

The small amount of dough goes a long way because it's rolled so thin. There are thicker versions from other parts of central Asia, as well as super-thin cracker versions (see page 133). We pull our lavash from the oven when only lightly browned and still chewy. Like so many other things, this is a matter of taste, so if you're looking for a cracker bread, bake it until deep brown and crispy. Experiment with several doughs—this a very versatile recipe.

Makes several lavash

¼ pound (plum-size portion) Olive Oil Dough (page 119), 100% Whole Wheat Bread
    dough (page 79), or Semolina Bread dough (page 89)
Olive oil, for rolling
Seeds, for sprinkling on the lavash
Coarse sea salt, for sprinkling on the lavash

1. Preheat the oven to 400°F, with a rack placed in the center of the oven.

2. Dust the surface of the refrigerated dough with flour and cut off a ¼-pound (plum-size) piece. Quickly shape it into a loose ball by stretching the surface of the dough around to the bottom, rotating the ball a quarter-turn as you go.

3. Place the dough on an 11 × 16-inch piece of oiled parchment paper and flatten the dough, using your hands. Drizzle more oil over the top of the dough and cover with plastic wrap. Use a rolling pin to evenly roll the dough until it is the size of the sheet of

parchment and as thin as possible. Make sure the dough is an even thickness through-out.

4. Peel off the plastic and sprinkle the dough with seeds and salt. Prick the surface all over with a fork to allow steam to escape and to prevent puffing. There's no need for resting time.

5. Slide the lavash-covered parchment paper directly onto a baking sheet and into the oven. Bake for about 5 minutes, or until lightly browned. Rotate and continue baking until evenly baked, but still soft.

6. Let cool briefly and serve warm. Once cool, it stores very well in plastic bags. Unlike hard-crusted breads, lavash is not harmed by airtight storage.

VARIATION: CRACKER LAVASH

Follow the recipe for Lavash but bake until crisp, an extra 5 to 10 minutes. Make sure it is baking evenly by rotating the baking sheet often as it bakes. Once the cracker has cooled, break it into pieces and serve, or present it whole and let people break off pieces on their own.

Semolina and Butter Swirl Bread (Moroccan Meloui)

Meloui are yeasted semolina pancakes from Morocco, and their many buttered layers make them flaky and full of air. These flatbreads are traditionally served during Ramadan or for breakfast any time of the year. They are usually served with honey, but you can experiment with your favorite toppings.

Makes one 12-inch flatbread

½ pound (orange-size portion) Semolina Bread dough (page 89)

All-purpose flour, for dusting

3 tablespoons butter, softened, plus more for rolling

1 ¼ teaspoons semolina, for sprinkling on the dough

Honey, for serving

1. To bake: Dust the surface of the refrigerated dough with flour and cut off a ½-pound (orange-size) piece. Dust with more flour and quickly shape it into a ball by stretching the surface of the dough around to the bottom, rotating the ball a quarter-turn as you go. Flatten with your fingers and a rolling pin into a ⅛-inch-thick rectangle, about 9 × 12 inches. If the dough is sticking, lightly grease with butter. It is easiest to do this on a silicone mat or a greased sheet of parchment paper, so it won't stick to the counter.

2. Evenly spread 2 tablespoons of the butter over the surface of the dough and sprinkle with 1 teaspoon of the semolina. Fold the dough in thirds, like a letter. Spread 1 teaspoon butter over the top of the folded dough and sprinkle with the remaining ¼ teaspoon semolina. Fold again into thirds, creating a very thin rectangle. Roll the dough into a rope and stretch it until it is about 24 inches long. Coil the rope tightly around

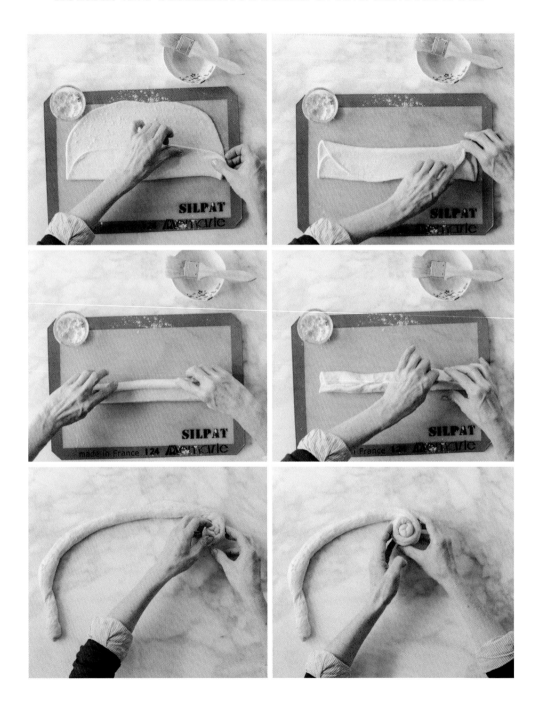

itself. Place on a work surface lightly greased with butter or olive oil, cover loosely with plastic wrap, and allow to rest at room temperature for 40 minutes.

3. Once the dough has rested, roll the coil out on a lightly oiled surface until you have a ⅛-inch-thick round about 12 inches wide.

4. Heat a heavy 12-inch skillet over medium-high heat until water droplets flicked into the pan skitter across the surface and evaporate quickly. Add the remaining 2 teaspoons butter.

5. Drop the rolled-out dough into the skillet, decrease the heat to medium, and cook for about 3 minutes, or until the bottom is nicely browned. Flip the dough when the underside is richly browned. Continue cooking another 2 to 5 minutes, or until the flatbread feels firm and even at the edges, and the second side is browned. (You'll need more pan time if you've rolled a thicker bread.)

6. Allow to cool slightly on a rack; then, drizzle with honey, break it apart, and enjoy.

Matzo

Jews eat matzo during the festival of Passover to commemorate their ancestors' flight from slavery, when they left Egypt so suddenly that their bread had no time to rise. Matzo serves as a reminder of the continued struggle for justice in the world. Unfortunately, the bland taste of these flat sheets tends to be reminiscent of cardboard. But that doesn't have to be the case if you make your own. Matzo is one of the easiest and fastest flatbreads there is, because there is no yeast to wait on. In fact, it is dictated by Jewish tradition that matzo be made in 18 minutes. The Israelites had that amount of time to flee Egypt. Obviously, this won't be kosher for Passover, but if you are okay with that, it is the BEST matzo you will ever eat and a great project to get your kids excited about the holiday.

Makes 6 large matzo

2 cups all-purpose flour

1 teaspoon kosher salt

1 tablespoon olive oil

¾ cup water

1. Preheat a baking stone to 500°F, with a rack placed in the center of the oven.

2. Set your timer for 18 minutes. For some, this will be a crucial part of the recipe and for others, it will just be fun to see if you can complete the project in that amount of time. It is important to have everything ready to go, so you don't waste any time gathering equipment or ingredients.

3. In a large bowl, mix the flour, salt, oil and water until a ball comes together.

4. Divide the ball into 6 pieces.

5. Roll each piece very, very thin. A heavy rolling pin works well for this, since you need to get the job done fast and you want it very thin. Way back in the day, matzo wasn't square, so just let the dough dictate the shape; we're just concerned about getting it as thin as possible.

6. Use a fork to poke the dough, so it won't puff too much in the oven.

7. Slide the dough onto the preheated baking stone using a pizza peel and bake for about 2 minutes, and then flip the dough to bake the other side. You will want to bake more than one at a time to get them all done within 18 minutes. Use two baking stones in the oven at one time, one at the bottom and one toward the top of the oven. If you have a double wall oven, then you are in great shape to get this done in time.

8. The matzo will be golden and crisp when it is done. Let it cool on a rack.

Persian New Year Bread (Koloocheh)

At the end of March, Persian families celebrate thirteen days of *Nowruz*, a festival marking the spring equinox and the first day of the Iranian calendar. Nowruz is a time for house-cleaning, bonfires, gifts, and of course, indulgent feasts with holiday visitors. It is customary to decorate an elaborate table with symbolic items like greenery, books, and coins before laying out the dishes. This Persian New Year Bread is inspired by the cookie of the same name and is a favorite Nowruz treat, also known as *koloocheh*. The pattern on top of the koloocheh looks like a flower, a perfect symbol of rebirth and springtime, and is traditionally created with an embossed stamp. You can find a close replication of the stamps at Nordic Ware, sold as cookie stamps. No matter the time of year, these golden sweets will fill your house will a perfume of nuts and spices.

Makes eight 4-inch pastries

¾ cup walnuts

½ cup confectioners' sugar

1½ teaspoons ground cinnamon

1 pound (grapefruit-size portion) Yogurt Challah dough (page 151), Challah dough (page 147), Brioche dough (page 65), Semolina Bread dough (page 89), or any other enriched dough in the book

All-purpose flour, for dusting

Egg yolk wash (1 yolk beaten with 1 tablespoon water), for brushing the pastries

1. Preheat the oven to 350°F, with a rack placed in the center of the oven.

2. In a food processor, pulverize the walnuts, confectioners' sugar, and cinnamon until powdery.

3. Dust the surface of the refrigerated dough with flour and cut off a 1-pound (grapefruit-size) piece. Divide the dough into 8 equal pieces. Dust each piece with more flour and quickly shape it into a ball by stretching the surface of the dough around to the bottom, rotating the ball a quarter-turn as you go. Place the dough on a flour-dusted surface.

4. Using your hands and a rolling pin, roll 1 ball of dough out into a ¼-inch-thick round, about 4 inches wide. Place 2 teaspoons of the walnut filling in the middle. Pinch the dough around it, like a purse. Flip the purse over, gathered side down, and roll until it is 4 inches wide again. Place the dough on a baking sheet lined with parchment paper. Repeat with the remaining dough and filling.

5. Create a design in the dough using a koloocheh stamp or the rounded edge of a small round cutter, dipped in flour, to create circles. You want to make an impression in the dough, but not cut through it. Once you've created your design, go over the pattern with a fork. This will prevent the dough from puffing and ruining your design.

6. Brush lightly with egg yolk wash.

7. Bake for about 20 minutes, or until caramel brown.

8. Allow to cool slightly on a rack before serving.

9

CHALLAH AND BABKA

Every Friday at sundown, Jewish households welcome the Sabbath, a time of rest, reflection, and rejuvenation. Families celebrate the end of the workweek with comforting meals, which traditionally include two loaves of challah. According to some traditions, the braided strands symbolize the bonds of love. When you break through the soft golden-brown crust, you find a white, pillowy interior.

On Rosh Hashanah, the Jewish New Year, the challah is often shaped into a round coil to resemble a turban. This represents continuity and the natural cycles of time. For a simpler but still festive take, try connecting the ends of a normal braided challah to form a wreath shape. Once you get the hang of the traditional three-strand braid, experiment with four- and six-strand braids, or even a triple-stacked challah, with smaller braids stacked on top of a larger one.

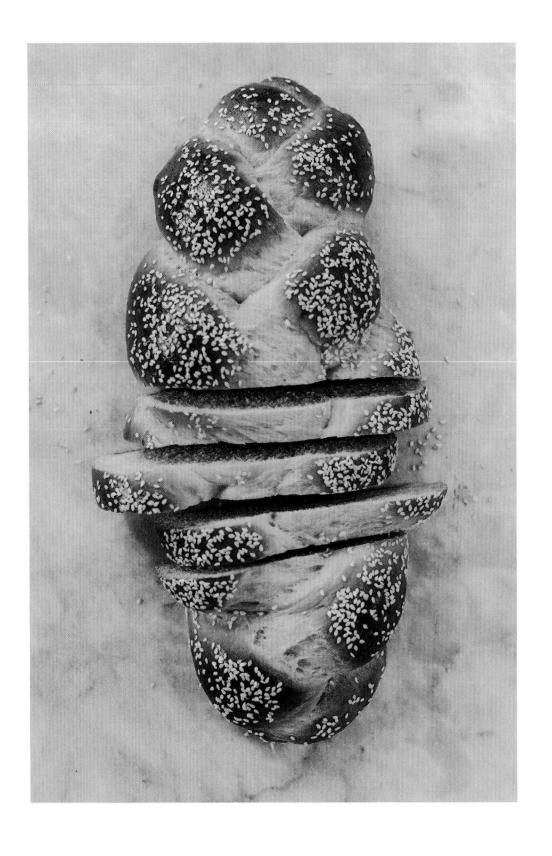

Challah (Three-Strand Braid)

Challah is traditionally baked on Fridays in Jewish households, and it symbolizes the start of the Sabbath, a time of rest. It's enriched with eggs and sweetened just enough to make an ordinary Friday feel like a holiday.

We also include variations on the traditional three-strand braid. With a little practice, you'll have no trouble plaiting three, four, and even six strands of dough (see pages 155–162) to create a gorgeous challah. And if you're strapped for oven space try a round challah in the crock pot (page 151).

This dough made with a bit of yogurt (see variation) gives it a wonderful tang and richness that is wonderful used in the Bosphorus Pita (page 123), the Persian New Year Bread (page 141), and many other loaves.

The Challah dough is the foundation for our flaky Danish Dough on page 334.

Makes four loaves, slightly less than 1 pound each. The recipe is easily doubled or halved.

INGREDIENT	VOLUME (U.S.)	WEIGHT (U.S.)	WEIGHT (METRIC)
Lukewarm water (100°F or below)	1¾ cups	14 ounces	400 grams
Granulated yeast[1]	1 tablespoon	0.35 ounce	10 grams
Kosher salt[1]	1 tablespoon	0.6 ounce	17 grams
Large eggs, lightly beaten	4	8 ounces	225 grams
Honey	½ cup	6 ounces	170 grams
Unsalted butter, melted (can substitute oil or melted margarine)	8 tablespoons (1 stick)	4 ounces	115 grams
Bread flour	7 cups	2 pounds, 3 ounces	990 grams
Egg yolk wash (1 egg yolk beaten with 1 tablespoon water), for brushing the loaf[2]			
Poppy or sesame seeds, for sprinkling on the loaf			

[1] Can decrease (see pages 15 and 33).

[2] See page 40 for other options.

1. Mixing and storing the dough: Mix the water, yeast, salt, eggs, honey, and melted butter in a 6-quart bowl or a lidded (not airtight) food container.

2. Mix in the flour without kneading, using a heavy-duty stand mixer (with paddle), a Danish dough whisk, or a spoon. If you're not using a machine, you may need to use wet hands to incorporate the last bit of flour.

3. Cover (not airtight) and allow to rest at room temperature until the dough rises for 2 hours.

4. The dough can be used immediately after the initial rise, though it is easier to handle when cold. Refrigerate the container and use over the next 5 days. To freeze dough, see page 42.

5. On baking day, line a baking sheet with parchment paper or a silicone mat. Dust the surface of the refrigerated dough with flour and cut off a 1-pound (grapefruit-size) piece. Divide the dough into 3 equal pieces. Dust each piece with more flour and quickly shape into a ball by stretching the surface of the dough around to the bottom, rotating the ball a quarter-turn as you go.

6. Gently roll and stretch each dough ball, dusting with flour so your hands don't stick to it, until you have a long rope about ¾ inch thick, about 15 inches long. You may need to let the dough relax for 5 minutes so it won't resist your efforts.

7. Braid the challah: Lay the 3 ropes side by side and, starting from the middle of the loaf, pull the left strand (rope) over the center strand and lay it down; always pull the outer strands into the middle, never moving what becomes the center strand.

8. Now pull the right strand over the center strand. Continue, alternating outer strands, but always pulling into the center. When you get to the end, pinch the strands together.

9. Flip the challah over so that the loose strands fan away from you. Start braiding again by pulling an outside strand to the middle, but this time *start with the right strand*. Braid to the end again, and pinch the strands together.

Visit BreadIn5.com, where you'll find recipes, photos, videos, and instructional material.

149

10. If the braid is oddly shaped, fix it by nudging and stretching. Place on the prepared baking sheet, cover loosely with plastic wrap, and allow to rest at room temperature for 90 minutes.

11. Preheat the oven to 350°F, with a rack placed in the center of the oven. Brush the loaf with egg yolk wash and sprinkle with the seeds.

12. Bake for about 30 minutes. Smaller or larger loaves will require adjustments in baking time. The challah is done when golden brown, and the braid near the center of the loaf is set.

13. Allow to cool on a rack before slicing and eating.

BRAIDING FROM ONE END: You can braid starting at the end of the loaf and go all the way to the other end, but starting in the middle (and flipping) makes for a more even loaf all the way along.

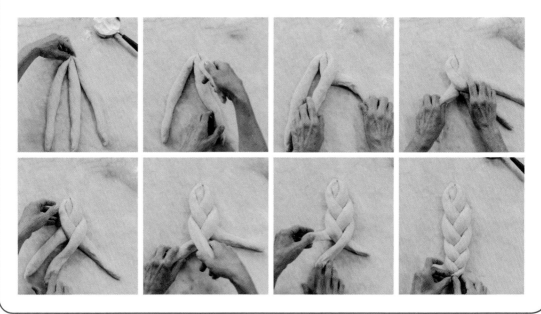

VARIATION: YOGURT CHALLAH

Using yogurt in dough is very common in the Middle East and India. There are several breads in the book where we recommend this version, but it's great used in just about any recipe calling for challah.

Follow the recipe for Challah, replacing ¾ cup of the water with room-temperature yogurt.

VARIATION: CROCK POT CHALLAH

Braid a 3-strand braid, then join the 2 ends to form a circle. Place it on a piece of parchment paper and bake as directed in Crock Pot Bread (page 54).

Whole-Grain Challah Dough

Here's a delicious and nutritious braided loaf with all the classic flavors of challah: eggs, poppy seeds, and honey. Vegetable oils make a great vegan challah, including coconut oil, which also lends nice flavor. No change is needed in the recipe, but if you go with coconut oil, you'll need to melt in the microwave or on the stove first, and be aware that dough made with coconut oil will seem drier and "tighter" than doughs made with the other fats. Don't worry—it bakes up beautifully.

This dough can make all of the beautiful challahs in this chapter.

Makes enough dough for at least five 1-pound loaves. The recipe is easily doubled or halved.

INGREDIENT	VOLUME (U.S.)	WEIGHT (U.S.)	WEIGHT (METRIC)
Whole wheat flour	5 cups	1 pound, 6½ ounces	640 grams
All-purpose flour	3 cups	15 ounces	425 grams
Granulated yeast[1]	1 tablespoon	0.35 ounce	10 grams
Kosher salt[1]	1 tablespoon	0.6 ounce	17 grams
Lukewarm water (100°F or below)	2¾ cups	1 pound, 6 ounces	625 grams
Honey	½ cup	6 ounces	170 grams
Vegetable oil, melted coconut oil, or butter	¼ cup	2 ounces	55 grams
Large eggs, lightly beaten	4	8 ounces	230 grams
Pure vanilla extract	1 teaspoon		
Egg wash (1 egg beaten with 1 tablespoon water), for brushing the loaf			
Poppy or sesame seeds, for sprinkling on the loaf			

[1]Can decrease (see pages 15 and 33).

1. Mixing and storing the dough: Whisk together the flours, yeast, and salt in a 5-quart bowl or a lidded (not airtight) food container.

2. Combine the water, honey, oil, and eggs. Add them to the dry ingredients without kneading using a heavy duty stand mixer (with paddle), a Danish dough whisk, or a spoon. You might need to use wet hands to get the last bit of flour to incorporate if you're not using a machine.

3. Cover (not airtight) and allow the dough to rest at room temperature until it rises for 2 hours.

4. The dough can be used immediately after its initial rise, though it is easier to handle when cold. Refrigerate it in a lidded (not airtight) container and use over the next 5 days. To freeze dough, see page 42.

Four-Strand Round Braided Challah

Makes 1 challah

1½ pounds (small cantaloupe–size portion) Challah dough (page 147) or Whole-Grain
   Challah Dough (page 152)
Flour, for dusting
Egg yolk wash (1 egg yolk beaten with 1 tablespoon water)

1. To bake: Line a baking sheet with parchment paper or a silicone mat. Dust the surface of the refrigerated dough with flour and cut off a 1½-pound (small cantaloupe–size) piece. Divide the dough into 4 equal pieces. Form each piece into an 18-inch rope.

2. Place 2 ropes side by side, and then weave the other 2 ropes over and under them at the middle. The 4 ropes will form a cross, with 2 strands heading north, east, south, and west.

3. Start by taking the strand to the left and cross it over the right one, always going clockwise. Do this with all 4 strands.

4. Now cross the strand that was the right (under the left one) and cross it over the left one, this time going counter clockwise. Do this with all 4 pairs of strands.

5. Repeat this process until the strands are too short to cross each other.

6. Finish by tucking the ends up under the loaf.

7. Place the braided challah on a baking sheet lined with parchment paper. Dust with a little flour and cover very loosely with plastic. Let the loaf rise for 90 minutes.

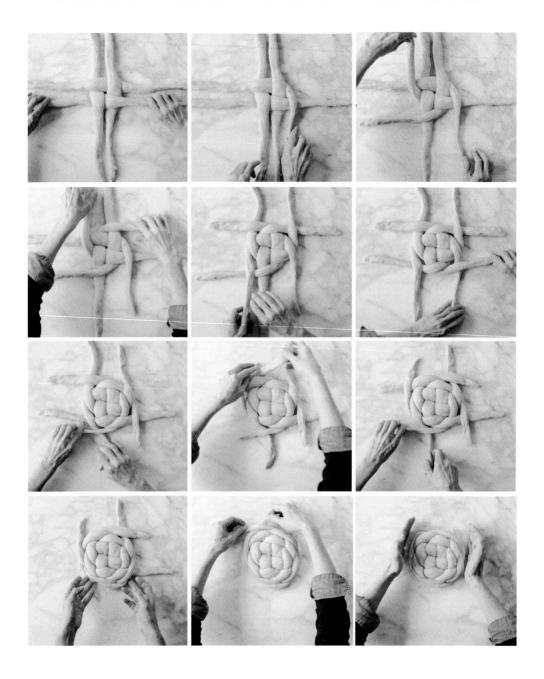

8. Preheat the oven to 350°F, with a rack placed in the center of the oven.

9. Brush the top of the loaf with egg yolk wash.

10. Bake for about 40 minutes, or until the loaf is golden brown and firm to the touch. Depending on how high versus how wide your braid is, you may need to bake it for an additional 5 to 10 minutes.

11. Allow the loaf to cool completely before serving.

Six-Strand Braided Challah

Makes I challah

2 pounds (cantaloupe-size portion) Challah dough (page 147), Whole-Grain Challah
   Dough (page 152), Brioche dough (page 65), or any other enriched dough
Flour, for dusting
Egg yolk wash (1 egg yolk beaten with 1 tablespoon water), for brushing the loaf
Sesame or poppy seeds, for sprinkling on the loaf

1. To bake: Line a baking sheet with parchment paper or a silicone mat. Dust the surface of the refrigerated dough with flour and cut off a 2-pound (cantaloupe-size) piece. Divide the dough into 6 equal pieces. Form each of the pieces into a 15-inch rope.

2. Lay the ropes side by side, and then join the 6 ropes at the top by pinching the ends together.

3. Start by taking the piece on the outer right-hand edge and draping it over the tops of all the ropes. Now bring the second piece on the left-hand side and fold that into the middle.

4. These first few steps get things going, and then you will start to see a pattern form.

5. Take the second piece on the left-hand side and drape it over the top.

6. Take the top piece on the left-hand side and bring that to the middle.

7. Take the second piece on the right-hand side and drape that over the top.

8. Take the top piece on the right-hand side and bring it to the middle.

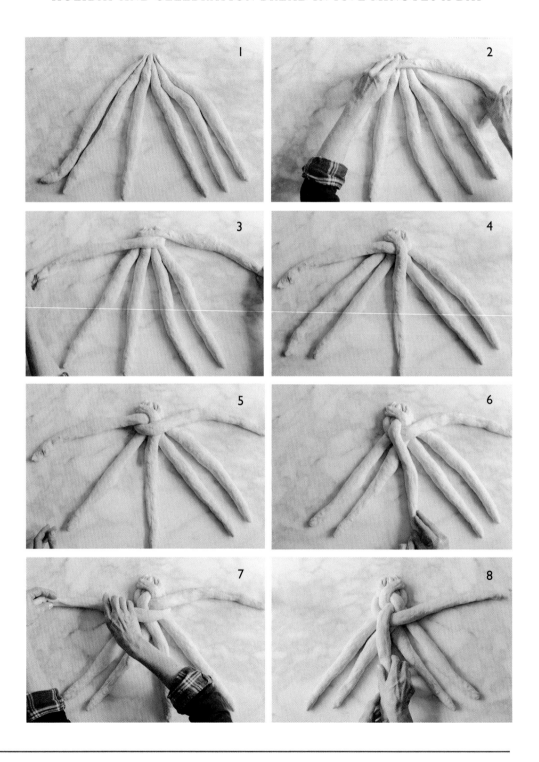

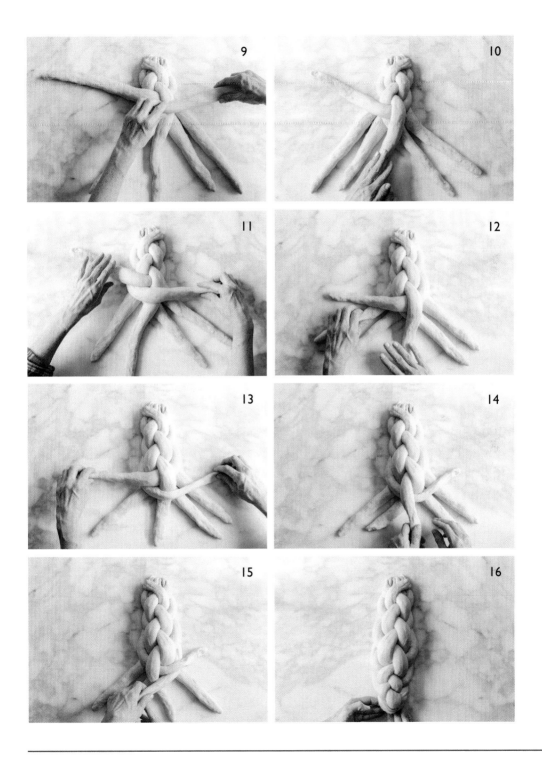

Visit BreadIn5.com, where you'll find recipes, photos, videos, and instructional material.

161

9. Take the second piece on the left-hand side and drape it over the top.

10. Continue by taking the top right-hand piece to the middle and then the second left-hand piece over the top. Then the top left-hand piece to the middle and the second right-hand piece to over the top and so on.

11. When you get to the bottom, it will become a bit trickier to work with the short pieces, but don't worry.

12. You will end up tucking them up under the end, so no one will ever know if you have to cheat a little.

13. Place the braided challah on a baking sheet lined with parchment paper. Dust with a little flour and cover very loosely with plastic. Allow to rise for 90 minutes.

14. Preheat the oven to 350°F, with a rack placed in the center of the oven.

15. Brush the top of the loaf with egg wash and sprinkle with seeds (if using).

16. Bake for about 40 minutes, or until the loaf is golden brown and firm to the touch. Depending on how high versus how wide your braid is, you may need to bake it for an additional 5 to 10 minutes.

17. Allow the loaf to cool completely before serving.

Stacked Challah Braids with a Twist

Makes I challah

1¾ pounds Challah dough (page 147), Whole-Grain Challah Dough (page 152), Brioche
  dough (page 65), or any other enriched dough in the book
Flour, for dusting
Egg yolk wash (1 egg yolk beaten with 1 tablespoon water), for brushing the loaf
Sesame or poppy seeds, for sprinkling on the loaf

1. To bake: Line a baking sheet with parchment paper or a silicone mat. Dust the surface of the refrigerated dough with flour and cut off a 1¾-pound (medium cantaloupe-size) piece. Divide the dough into 3 pieces (this is easiest done with a scale, but you can do it by eyeballing the different sized pieces as well).

> 1-pound (grapefruit-size) piece
> ½-pound (peach-size) piece
> ¼-pound (plum-size) piece

2. Start by dividing the 1-pound piece into 3 equal balls, and then stretch those pieces into ropes and braid them, just as the Challah recipe instructs (pages 147–148). Place the braid on a baking sheet lined with parchment paper.

3. Create a braid with the ½-pound piece of dough.

4. Divide the ¼-pound piece into 2 equal pieces, elongate them into ropes (about ½ inch wide), and then twist them together.

5. Stack the ½-pound braid on top of the 1-pound braid and then top with the ¼-pound twist.

6. Dust the loaf with a little flour and cover very loosely with plastic. Let the loaf rise for 90 minutes.

7. Preheat the oven to 350°F, with a rack placed in the center of the oven.

8. Brush the top of the loaf with egg wash and sprinkle with seeds (if using).

9. Bake for about 40 minutes, or until the loaf is golden brown and firm to the touch. Depending on how high versus how wide your braid is, you may need to bake it for an additional 5 to 10 minutes.

10. Allow the loaf to cool completely before serving.

Turban-Shaped Challah with Raisins

Turban-shaped raisin challah is served at the Jewish New Year, but similar enriched and fruited egg breads are part of holiday traditions all over the Western world, calling to mind the richer Italian panettone, served at Christmas (page 224).

We've assumed in this recipe that you're using stored dough and rolling the raisins into it. If you're starting a batch of dough just for raisin challah, add 2 cups of raisins to the yeasted water when mixing.

Makes 1 raisin challah

1 pound (grapefruit-size portion) Challah dough (page 147), Amish-Style Milk Bread dough
   (page 83), or Brioche dough (page 65), or any other enriched dough in the book
All-purpose flour, for dusting
½ cup raisins
Egg wash (1 egg beaten with 1 tablespoon water), for brushing the loaf
Sesame seeds, for sprinkling on the loaf

1. To bake: Line a baking sheet with parchment paper or a silicone mat. Dust the surface of the refrigerated dough with flour and cut off a 1-pound (grapefruit-size) piece. Dust the piece with more flour and quickly shape it into a ball by stretching the surface of the dough around to the bottom, rotating the ball a quarter-turn as you go.

2. Using a rolling pin and minimal dusting flour, roll out the dough to a thickness of ½ inch. Sprinkle with the raisins and roll into a log. (See page 171 for process photos.)

3. Rolling the dough between your hands and stretching it, form a single long, thin rope about 15 inches long, tapering it at one end. If the dough resists shaping, let it rest for 5 minutes and try again.

4. Starting with the thick end of the rope, begin forming a coil on the prepared baking sheet. When you have finished coiling, pinch the thin end under the loaf. Cover loosely with plastic wrap and allow to rest at room temperature for 90 minutes.

5. Preheat the oven to 350°F, with a rack placed in the center of the oven.

6. Brush the loaf with egg wash and sprinkle with seeds, and place near the center of the oven. Bake for about 30 to 35 minutes. The challah is done when golden brown and the center of the loaf offers resistance to pressure. Smaller or larger loaves will require adjustments in baking time.

7. Allow to cool on a rack before serving.

VARIATION: APPLE TURBAN

Instead of raisins, add ½ cup chopped apples (skin on and cut into ¼-inch dice) in step 2.

Tahini Swirl Bread

"Ground sesame paste (tahini) *has been popular for hundreds of years from the eastern Mediterranean region throughout the Middle East and into Northern Africa. I grew up on a commune in northern Vermont in the 1960s, and tahini was a staple in our diet. It was delicious, nutritious, and super versatile. Mostly I remember eating it slathered on toasted homemade bread, but we also made it into hummus and salad dressing. Recently, it's become the darling of food bloggers and is found in lots of foods and desserts. This tahini bread is rich, slightly sweet, and full of flavor."* —Zoë

Makes 1 swirled loaf

   1 pound (grapefruit-size portion) Challah dough (page 147), Whole-Grain Challah Dough
      (page 152), Brioche dough (page 65), or any enriched dough in the book
¾ cup tahini
¼ cup sugar
2 teaspoons ground cinnamon
All-purpose flour, for dusting
½ cup chopped walnuts
Egg yolk wash (1 yolk beaten with 1 tablespoon water), for brushing the loaf
Sesame seeds, for sprinkling on the loaf

1. To bake: Grease an 8-inch cake pan. Dust the surface of the refrigerated dough with flour and cut off a 1-pound (grapefruit-size) piece. Dust the piece with more flour and quickly shape it into a ball by stretching the surface of the dough around to the bottom, rotating the ball a quarter-turn as you go.

2. Make the tahini filling: Mix the tahini, sugar, and cinnamon in a bowl.

3. Using a rolling pin and minimal dusting flour, roll the dough out into a ¼-inch-thick rectangle, about 9 × 12 inches. Spread the tahini filling over the dough, sprinkle on the walnuts, and roll into a log.

4. Rolling the dough between your hands and stretching it, form a rope about 12 inches long, tapering it slightly at the ends. Form the rope into a coil and secure the end under the loaf. Place the coil in the prepared pan. Cover loosely with plastic wrap and allow to rest at room temperature for 90 minutes.

5. Preheat the oven to 350°F, with a rack placed in the center of the oven.

6. Brush the loaf with egg wash, sprinkle with seeds, and place near the center of the oven. Bake for 35 to 40 minutes. The tahini swirl is done when golden brown and the center of the loaf offers resistance to pressure. Smaller or larger loaves will require adjustments in baking time.

7. Allow to cool on a rack before serving.

Chocolate-Raisin Babka Bundt

It's not a typo—there really are sixteen yolks in this recipe, and we cut that back by half from the original Ukrainian recipe we were inspired by. This dough is super rich and decadent; it's best described as luxurious. You can make a twisted or Bundt-shaped babka by using any of our other doughs, but you should try this one on a special occasion.

Makes at least three 1½-pound loaves. The recipe is easily doubled or halved.

INGREDIENT	VOLUME (U.S.)	WEIGHT (U.S.)	WEIGHT (METRIC)
Lukewarm water (100°F or below)	3 cups	1 pound, 8 ounces	680 grams
Egg yolks	16	1 pound	455 grams
Granulated yeast[1]	1 tablespoon	0.35 ounce	10 grams
Sugar	½ cup	3½ ounces	100 grams
Kosher salt[1]	1 tablespoon	0.6 ounce	17 grams
Unsalted butter, melted, plus more for greasing the pan	12 tablespoons (1½ sticks)	6 ounces	170 grams
All-purpose flour	7½ cups	2 pounds, 5½ ounces	1,065 grams
Raisins, per loaf	¾ cup	4½ ounces	130 grams
Bittersweet chocolate, melted, per loaf	¾ cup	4½ ounces	130 grams
Rum, for soaking the baked loaf (optional), per loaf	¼ cup	2 ounces	55 grams

[1]Can decrease (see pages 15 and 33).

1. Mixing and storing the dough: Mix the milk, egg yolks, yeast, sugar, salt, and melted butter in a 6-quart bowl or a lidded (not airtight) food container.

2. Mix in the flour without kneading, using a heavy-duty stand mixer (with paddle), a Danish dough whisk, or a spoon. The mixture will be quite loose because of all the yolks.

3. Cover (not airtight) and allow to rest at room temperature until the dough rises for 2 hours.

4. The dough will be loose, but will firm up when chilled. Don't try to use it without chilling for at least 3 hours. Refrigerate the container and use over the next 5 days. To freeze dough, see page 42.

5. On baking day, grease a Bundt pan or an 8½ × 4½-inch nonstick loaf pan with butter. Dust the surface of the refrigerated dough with flour and cut off a 1½-pound (cantaloupe-size) piece. Dust the piece with more flour and quickly shape it into a ball by stretching the surface of the dough around to the bottom, rotating the ball a quarter-turn as you go.

6. Using a rolling pin, roll the dough out into a ¼-inch-thick rectangle, about 11 × 15 inches. Melt the chocolate and spread it evenly over the dough and sprinkle the raisins over it. Roll the dough into a log, starting at the long end, and pinch the seam closed. Place the dough in the prepared pan. Cover loosely with plastic wrap and allow to rest at room temperature for 90 minutes.

7. Preheat the oven to 350°F, with a rack placed in the center of the oven.

8. Bake for 45 minutes, or until golden brown and firm. Brush with rum immediately (if using).

9. Allow to cool on a rack before serving.

VARIATION: TWISTED BABKA

Follow the Chocolate-Raisin Babka Bundt recipe, but use a knife or bench scraper to cut down the length of the rope, exposing the filling. Keeping the filling facing upward, twist the 2 long pieces. Tuck the 2 ends under and place the twist in the prepared pan (see the Lemon Curd Twist photo on page 177 for instructions).

Lemon Curd Twist

Lemon curd is often served as a spread, but in this bread it is swirled into the dough so you get a bit of tart zing in every bite. This twist is a wonderful way to add flavors to your bread and it is so pretty. Try the Coconut Chocolate Twist (page 178) or get creative with your own fillings.

Makes 1 loaf

I pound (grapefruit-size portion) Babka dough (page 173), Challah dough (page 147),
    or any other enriched dough in the book
All-purpose flour, for dusting
¾ cup Lemon Curd (page 356)
Streusel (page 303) with ½ teaspoon grated lemon zest added to it

1. To bake: Generously grease a parchment-lined 8½ × 4½-inch nonstick loaf pan. Dust the surface of the refrigerated dough with flour and cut off a 1-pound (grapefruit-size) piece. Dust the piece with more flour and quickly shape it into a rough ball by stretching the surface of the dough around to the bottom, rotating the ball a quarter-turn as you go.

2. Roll the dough out to a ⅛-inch-thick rectangle, about 12 × 15 inches. As you roll out the dough, add flour as needed to prevent sticking.

3. Spread the lemon curd evenly over the dough. Sprinkle three-quarters of the streusel over the curd.

4. Starting with the long side of the dough, roll it up into a log. Pinch the seam closed. Stretch the log until it is about 2 inches thick. Cut the log in half, lengthwise. Twist the

Visit BreadIn5.com, where you'll find recipes, photos, videos, and instructional material.

175

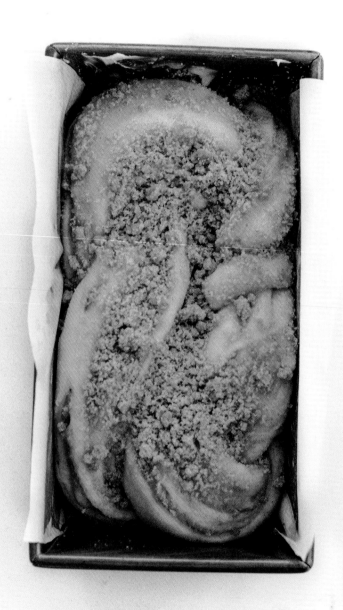

2 long pieces together, with the cut side facing up. Form an oval with the ends together and place in the prepared pan.

5. Cover loosely with plastic wrap and allow to rest at room temperature for 90 minutes.

6. Preheat the oven to 350°F, with a rack placed in the center of the oven.

---

7. Sprinkle the loaf with the remaining streusel.

8. Bake the loaf for about 45 minutes, or until golden brown and well set.

9. Allow to cool on a rack completely before eating (good luck with that!).

VARIATION:
COCONUT CHOCOLATE TWIST

This is like having a candy bar twisted into a loaf—umm, yes, thank you! You'll want to eat this warm from the oven, while the filling is still gooey.

    4 tablespoons (½ stick) butter, melted
    ½ cup sugar
    ½ cup well-packed shredded coconut
    ¼ teaspoon salt
    ¼ cup sweetened condensed milk
    1 teaspoon pure vanilla extract
    ½ cup chopped chocolate (any kind you like)

Mix all the ingredients together in a bowl. Follow the directions for the Lemon Curd Twist, but replace the lemon curd with the coconut mixture and omit the streusel. Rest and bake as instructed.

10

GOOEY, STICKY GOODNESS

Sticky Caramel Nut Rolls

Our Pecan Sticky Rolls are probably the most popular sweet bread from our past books, and we predict this version will end up with the same reputation. This recipe makes a big batch, because if you don't make a bunch of them, you end up regretting it. Make sure you have a deep enough pan, or your caramel will try to escape, so we recommend a 9-inch springform pan, because they are deeper than regular cake pans. You won't actually use the spring action unless the rolls get stuck, but they rarely do.

We went a little crazy with the nuts, using a mix of almonds, pecans, and walnuts. You can use just about any mix you want, or stick to just one kind.

Makes 8 large caramel rolls

12 tablespoons (1½ sticks) unsalted butter, melted, plus more for greasing the pan

1¼ cups well-packed brown sugar

¼ cup honey

1 teaspoon ground cinnamon

¼ teaspoon freshly grated nutmeg

½ teaspoon salt

Pinch freshly ground black pepper

1 cup pecan halves, toasted

1 cup walnut halves, toasted

1 cup whole almonds, toasted

1½ pounds (small cantaloupe–size portion) Amish-Style Milk Bread dough (page 83),
    Challah dough (page 147), Brioche dough (page 65), White Bread Master Recipe dough
    (page 48), or any other dough in the book

All-purpose flour, for dusting

1. To bake: Mix together the melted butter, brown sugar, honey, cinnamon, nutmeg, salt, and pepper. Grease the sides of a 9 × 3-inch springform cake pan with butter. (If your pan doesn't have a great seal, then line the bottom and sides of the pan with a piece of parchment paper and grease the parchment.) Spread half the butter-sugar mixture evenly over the bottom. Scatter half the pecans, walnuts, and almonds over the butter-sugar mixture and set aside.

2. Dust the surface of the refrigerated dough with flour and cut off a 1½-pound (small cantaloupe–size) piece. Dust the piece with more flour and quickly shape it into a ball by stretching the surface of the dough around to the bottom, rotating the ball a quarter-turn as you go.

3. Using a rolling pin, roll the dough out into a ⅛-inch-thick rectangle, about 14 × 8 inches. As you roll out the dough, use enough flour to prevent it from sticking to the work surface, but not so much as to make the dough dry.

4. Spread the remaining butter-sugar mixture evenly over the rolled-out dough, chop the remaining nuts, and sprinkle them over the top. Starting with the long side, roll the dough into a log and pinch the seam shut.

5. With a very sharp serrated knife or kitchen shears, cut the log into 8 equal pieces and arrange over the nuts in the pan, so that the swirled cut edge is facing down. Cover loosely with plastic wrap and allow to rest at room temperature for 1 hour.

6. Preheat the oven to 350°F, with a rack placed in the center of the oven.

7. Place the pan on a baking sheet, in case the caramel bubbles over, and bake for about 40 minutes, or until golden brown and well set in center. While still hot, run a knife around the edge of the pan to release the rolls and invert immediately onto a serving dish. If you let them set too long, they will stick to the pan and be difficult to turn out.

8. Allow to cool for about 15 minutes before serving.

REFRIGERATOR RISE: Set your caramel nut rolls up the night before, so you can bake them first thing in the morning: Prepare the rolls, cover loosely with plastic, and refrigerate for up to 18 hours. When ready to bake, preheat the oven and then slide the rolls into the oven. They will take longer to bake, since they will be chilled. They've had a long, slow rise in the refrigerator, so you don't need to let them rise more before baking. This method works well for most of the breads in this book.

Cinnamon Rolls (All the Ways)

Versions of the cinnamon roll can be traced to Denmark and Sweden, but they have taken on a life of their own in the United States. A day isn't complete without seeing the fluffy spiral buns, filled with cinnamon sugar and butter, slathered with icing on Instagram. They've become synonymous with a joy-filled breakfast; a fresh batch is the perfect way to kick your mornings up a notch. Try all the fun variations.

Makes 6 cinnamon rolls

1 pound (grapefruit-size portion) Brioche dough (page 65), Amish-Style Milk Bread dough (page 83), Chocolate Bread dough (page 85), Pumpkin Pie Bread dough (page 71), or any other enriched dough in the book

All-purpose flour, for dusting

2 tablespoons unsalted butter, melted (plus more for greasing the pan, if using one)

¼ cup granulated sugar

¼ cup well-packed brown sugar

Pinch salt

1½ teaspoons ground cinnamon (or add some zing and use Chinese five-spice powder instead)

½ teaspoon grated orange zest

CREAM CHEESE ICING

4 ounces cream cheese, at room temperature

3 tablespoons confectioners' sugar

2 tablespoons heavy cream

½ teaspoon pure vanilla extract

¼ teaspoon grated orange zest

1. Dust the surface of the refrigerated dough with flour and cut off a 1-pound (grapefruit-size) piece. Dust the piece with more flour and quickly shape it into a ball by stretching the surface of the dough around to the bottom, rotating the ball a quarter-turn as you go.

2. Using a rolling pin, roll the dough out into a ¼-inch-thick rectangle, about 9 × 12 inches. As you roll out the dough, use just enough flour to prevent it from sticking to the work.

3. Brush the melted butter onto the entire surface.

4. In a small bowl, mix together the sugars, salt, cinnamon, and orange zest. Spread the mixture over the butter-topped dough. Use your hands to make sure you have an even coat of the sugar.

5. Roll the dough up, starting at the short end.

6. Cut the log into 6 equal pieces.

7. Set the buns on a baking sheet lined with parchment paper or in a buttered 9-inch baking dish. If you're baking on a sheet, leave 1½ to 2 inches between them. It's okay if they touch in the oven.

8. Cover loosely with plastic wrap and allow to rest at room temperature for 75 minutes.

9. Preheat the oven to 350°F, with a rack placed in the center of the oven.

10. Bake for 25 to 30 minutes, just until the centers are set when poked with your finger. They should be caramel colored.

11. Allow them to cool for about 10 minutes.

12. Make the cream cheese icing: Mix together the ingredients for the icing and spread over the warm buns. Enjoy!

VARIATION: MINI CINNAMON ROLLS

Makes 12 rolls

Follow the Cinnamon Rolls recipe, but stretch the log to be 1½ inches wide and cut it into 12 rolls. Set them in a buttered baking dish. Cover and allow to rest for 45 minutes. Bake for about 20 minutes, or until just set. Cool and frost as directed.

VARIATION: CROCK POT CINNAMON ROLLS

Makes 8 rolls

Follow the Cinnamon Rolls recipe but cut the log of dough into 8 pieces. Place the rolls close together on a piece of parchment paper, and drop them into a crock pot. Cook on high for about an hour. Depending on your machine, it may take more or less time to cook. Cool and frost as directed.

VARIATION: GINORMOUS SKILLET CINNAMON ROLL

Makes 1 ginormous roll

After you cover the dough with the cinnamon sugar filling, cut the dough into 1½-inch-wide strips. Roll one of the strips into a tight coil. Place the coil on the next strip and roll that strip around the coil, connecting the two ends together. Repeat with the remaining strips of dough until you have a giant coil of dough. At some point, you will have to lay the coil down and wind the dough around it, or it will get too large and unwieldy. Transfer the ginormous coil to a buttered  8-inch cast-iron skillet. Cover and allow to rest for 75 minutes. Bake at 350°F for about 35 minutes, until golden brown and set in the middle. Let it cool for 10 minutes, and then cover with cream cheese icing.

VARIATION: TRUCK STOP CINNAMON ROLLS (THEY'RE HUGE!)

Makes 8 large buns (sometimes bigger is better)

Follow the Cinnamon Rolls recipe, but cut the log of dough into 8 pieces, set them on a parchment-lined baking sheet, and allow to rest for 2 hours before baking. Bake for 35 to 40 minutes, or until set in the center and golden brown. Cool and frost as directed. Make a double batch of Cream Cheese Icing, and then cool and frost the rolls as directed.

VARIATION: JAMMIN' CINNAMON ROLLS

Follow the Cinnamon Rolls recipe, but omit the butter and instead spread ½ cup raspberry, blueberry, or cherry jam on the dough before adding the cinnamon sugar filling. Bake, cool, and frost as directed.

Chelsea Buns

The Chelsea Bun House in London was a celebrated bakery established around 1711. An unassuming building, it was filled with the finest art and décor and produced some of the most popular baked goods in London. It was even frequented by the royal family. The house specialty, the Chelsea bun, was essentially a currant- and raisin-studded cinnamon roll. (The Brits among you are rolling your eyes at that description, but it's meant as a true compliment.) The Chelsea Bun House closed in 1839, but a fresh Chelsea bun is sure to evoke the opulent regality of eighteenth-century England.

Makes 6 Chelsea buns

I pound (grapefruit-size portion) Brioche dough (page 65), Amish-Style Milk Bread dough
   (page 83), Challah dough (page 147), or any other enriched dough in the book
All-purpose flour, for dusting
4 tablespoons (½ stick) unsalted butter, melted
¼ cup granulated sugar
¼ cup well-packed brown sugar
I½ teaspoons ground cinnamon
¾ cup raisins

MILK GLAZE
½ cup confectioners' sugar
3 tablespoons milk
3 tablespoons demerara sugar

1. Dust the surface of the refrigerated dough with flour and cut off a 1-pound (grapefruit-size) piece. Dust the piece with more flour and quickly shape it into a ball by stretching the surface of the dough around to the bottom, rotating the ball a quarter-turn as you go.

2. Using a rolling pin, roll the dough out into a ¼-inch-thick rectangle, about 9 × 12 inches. As you roll out the dough, use enough flour to prevent it from sticking to the work surface but not so much as to make the dough dry.

3. Brush the melted butter onto the entire surface.

4. In a small bowl, mix together the sugars and cinnamon. Spread the mixture over the butter-topped dough. Use your hands to make sure you have an even coat of the sugar. Scatter the raisins over the dough.

5. Roll the dough up, starting at the long end.

6. Cut the log into 8 equal pieces.

7. Set the buns in a buttered 9-inch square baking dish. It's okay if they touch.

8. Cover loosely with plastic wrap and allow to rest at room temperature for 75 minutes.

9. Preheat the oven to 350°F, with a rack placed in the center of the oven.

10. Bake for 25 to 30 minutes, or just until the centers are set when poked with your finger. They should be light caramel colored.

11. Make the milk glaze: Mix together the ingredients for the glaze and spread over the warm buns. Sprinkle with the demerara sugar.

12. Eat while warm.

Twisted Cinnamon Buns

Makes 8 cinnamon buns

1½ pounds Amish-Style Milk Bread dough (page 83), Whole Wheat Brioche dough (page 68), or any other enriched dough in the book

⅓ cup well-packed brown sugar

⅓ cup granulated sugar

1 tablespoon ground cinnamon

All-purpose flour, for dusting

1. Mix together the brown sugar, granulated sugar, and cinnamon in a small bowl. Set aside.

2. Dust the surface of the refrigerated dough with flour and cut off a 1½-pound (cantaloupe-size) piece. Divide the dough into 8 equal pieces and quickly shape into balls.

3. Using a rolling pin and stretching with your hands, form 1 ball into a ¹⁄₁₆-inch-thick rectangle, about 4 × 12 inches.

4. Cover the dough with 2½ tablespoons of the cinnamon sugar, making sure it is evenly distributed and pressed into the dough.

5. Roll the dough up from the long end to make a 12-inch log.

6. Use the bench scraper to cut the log down the center, lengthwise.

7. Twist the 2 pieces together so the cinnamon sugar is exposed and you have a rope.

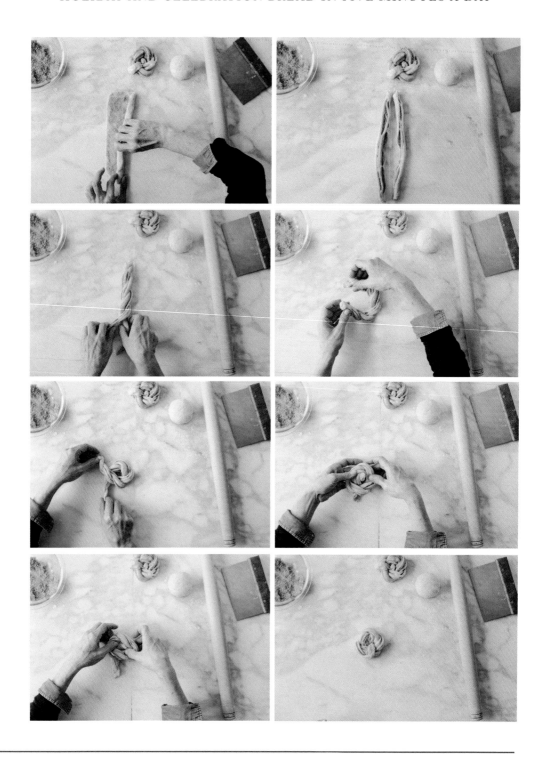

8. Tie the twisted rope into the knot. Place the knots on a baking sheet lined with parchment paper.

9. Repeat with the other pieces of dough.

10. Cover loosely with plastic wrap and allow to rest at room temperature for 1 hour.

11. Preheat the oven to 350°F, with a rack placed in the center of the oven.

12. Bake for about 20 minutes, or until set in the center when pressed.

13. Allow to cool for a few minutes, but they're terrific a little warm.

Cinnamon Twists and Turns

This is a great recipe for leftover scraps of rolled-out Brioche dough (page 65). You just make one or two as you are cutting scraps from another recipe or you can make dozens for a party. The end result may look a bit like modern art, but the flavor will be a real treat—wonderful with a cup of coffee.

> Scraps from Brioche dough (page 65) or any other enriched dough in the book
> ½ cup sugar
> 1 tablespoon ground cinnamon
> Egg wash (1 egg beaten with 1 tablespoon water), for brushing the twists

1. Line a baking sheet with parchment paper or a silicone mat.

2. Preheat the oven to 350°F, with a rack placed in the center of the oven.

3. Mix the sugar and cinnamon together in a small bowl. Set aside.

4. Brush the surface of the brioche scraps very lightly with egg wash, and sprinkle generously with the cinnamon sugar. Flip the scraps over and repeat on the opposite side.

5. Using a pizza cutter, cut the dough into ¾-inch strips or leave the scraps in odd shapes. Twist the strips into spirals and space evenly on the baking sheet. Let rest for 15 minutes. Depending on the size of the twists, they may turn in the oven and take on their own shape.

6. Bake for 15 to 20 minutes, or until golden brown. Serve warm.

Monkey Bread

Monkey bread has many origin stories, one of which starts out with pieces of dough dipped only in butter and baked in a cake pan from the 1940s. That nonsweet version, linked to the Parker House roll, was even served in the White House by Nancy Reagan. Other stories have the inspiration coming from the Hungarian-Jewish cinnamon coffee cake. No one knows for sure how a cake made from caramelized blobs of dough got its whimsical name, but it seems fitting, considering that monkey bread lets everyone play with their food, tearing off chunks like monkeys. One thing is certain: this is not a dessert for people who take themselves too seriously! If you're anything like us, you'll want to start pulling apart this loaf as soon as it comes out of the oven, but give it just a minute to cool off the molten caramel. This one is best served warm, while the caramel is still soft.

"I thought of making the leftovers into bread pudding, but there were no leftovers. I suggest you make two and use one in our bread pudding recipe (page 327)."—Zoë

Makes 1 monkey bread

1½ pounds (small cantaloupe-size portion) White Bread Master Recipe (page 48), Challah dough (page 147), Brioche dough (page 65), or any other enriched dough in the book

All-purpose flour, for dusting

8 tablespoons (1 stick) unsalted butter, plus more for greasing the pan

1 cup granulated sugar

1 tablespoon plus 1 teaspoon ground cinnamon

2 tablespoons brown sugar

¼ teaspoon salt

1 teaspoon pure vanilla extract

1. Generously butter a 9 × 5-inch loaf pan, Pullman pan, or Bundt pan.

2. Dust the surface of the refrigerated dough with flour and cut off a 1½-pound

(cantaloupe-size) piece. Divide the dough into about 32 equal pieces. Roll the dough into small balls. If the dough is sticking to your hands, coat your palms with a small amount of soft butter. Melt 4 tablespoons butter in a bowl. Combine the granulated sugar and cinnamon in a second bowl. Drop the dough balls into the butter and then coat them with the cinnamon sugar.

3. Place the balls in the prepared pan.

4. Allow the dough to rise for about 1 hour.

5. Preheat the oven to 350°F, with a rack placed in the center of the oven.

6. Just before putting the pan in the oven, melt the remaining 4 tablespoons butter, and then add any remaining cinnamon sugar, the brown sugar, the salt, and the vanilla. Pour over the dough balls.

7. Set the pan on a baking sheet, just in case the caramel bubbles over the top. Bake for about 40 minutes, or until caramelized and set.

8. Allow the bread to cool for about 5 minutes.

9. Invert the loaf onto a serving tray.

VARIATION: PECAN MONKEY BREAD

Add 1 cup pecan halves to the bottom of the pan after you pour in the caramel.

VARIATION: SPICED MONKEY BREAD

Play with the spices that you use. Try pumpkin pie spice blend, Chinese five-spice, or a blend of your favorites. If you use a super-intense spice, like cardamom, nutmeg, clove, allspice, or ginger, be sure to reduce it according to the intensity you want. Try starting with ½ teaspoon of some of those and build from there.

11

DOUGHNUTS

Fried dough can be found all over the world, in both savory and sweet forms. The ring-shaped doughnut, however, is a specifically American invention, one that we are forever grateful for. Dutch settlers in the sixteenth century brought *oliekoeken*, or "oily cakes," which were sweet and fried but had no hole and a rather unromantic name. In the early twentieth century, Russian immigrants introduced the doughnut machine to New York City and started mass-producing the fried rings, beginning a national craze. Since then, the humble doughnut has found a home in every region of the United States, evolving into a myriad of shapes and flavors. No matter the shape, doughnuts are always a smash hit with the whole family.

Along with the sweet fried treats, there are a couple of breads in this chapter that are on the savory side—an Italian ricotta fritter (page 216) and an Indian flatbread that puffs into a crisp cracker-like pita when it hits the oil (*bhatoora*, see page 219).

Honey-Glazed Doughnuts

The purest form of the doughnut, with nothing but a light honey glaze, because sometimes simplicity is best.

Makes twelve 3-inch doughnuts

> 1½ pounds (small cantaloupe–size portion) Amish-Style Milk Bread dough (page 83) or any other enriched dough in the book
>
> All-purpose flour, for dusting
>
> Neutral-flavored oil, for frying (use an oil with a high smoke point, like canola, peanut, or vegetable oil), enough to fill a deep saucepan 3 inches from the top

HONEY GLAZE

2 cups confectioners' sugar	¼ teaspoon pure vanilla extract
2 tablespoons honey	Pinch salt
2 tablespoons heavy cream	

1. Dust the surface of the refrigerated dough with flour and cut off a 1½-pound (small cantaloupe–size) piece. Dust the piece with more flour and quickly shape it into a ball by stretching the surface of the dough around to the bottom, rotating the ball a quarter-turn as you go.

2. Roll the dough out to a ¼-inch-thick rectangle, about 11 x 15 inches, on a lightly floured surface.

3. Have all of your equipment set out (see doughnut equipment sidebar, page 209). Heat the oil in a deep saucepan to 360°F to 370°F, as determined by a candy thermometer (see frying sidebar, page 203).

4. While the oil is heating, use a doughnut cutter to cut the dough into about 12 circles. Reserve the centers to fry as well. Return any scraps to the bucket of dough.

5. Drop the doughnuts in the hot oil two or three at a time so that they have plenty of room; they'll sink and then rise to the surface, where they will remain. Be careful not to overcrowd them, or they will not rise nicely.

6. After 1 minute, gently flip the doughnuts over with a slotted spoon and fry for another minute or so, or until golden brown on both sides.

7. Remove the doughnuts from the oil, and place them on paper towels to drain the extra oil. Repeat with the remaining dough until all the doughnuts are fried.

8. Make the honey glaze: Combine the confectioners' sugar, honey, cream, vanilla, and salt in a bowl and stir until smooth. Dip the doughnuts in the glaze. You can eat them immediately or let the glaze set up firm while you brew your coffee. You're welcome!

DOUGHNUT FRYING: Fried doughnuts don't become saturated with oil, so long as you fry them correctly. It's got to do with food's vapor pressure versus the oil's absorptive pressure, or to put it more plainly:

"If you fry at a high temperature (but not so high that it burns), the water inside the doughnut starts turning to steam immediately, and pushes out through pores in the developing doughnut crust. That outward movement prevents inward movement of oil. If you keep the temperature precisely where Zoë recommends, the finished weight of the doughnut will be remarkably close to where you started—it didn't absorb that much oil after all. After weighing a bunch of doughnuts before and after frying, and accounting for up to a 10 percent water loss in finished baked goods, our best estimate is that each doughnut only absorbs between 15 and 45 calories' worth of oil."—Jeff

EQUIPMENT FOR FRYING DOUGHNUTS: There are a few tools you'll need to make doughnuts. Nothing fancy, but having these on hand will make your doughnuts easier to make and as tasty as those from your favorite doughnut shop.

- A doughnut cutter or a 3-inch and 1-inch round biscuit/cookie cutters (the little one is for the doughnut holes).
- You need a deep saucepan for frying the oil. It needs to be deep enough that your doughnuts can float in the oil without being too close to the rim of the pan. You want at least three inches above the oil to be safe.
- A candy thermometer is a super easy way to keep track of how hot your oil is. Some people can look at the oil and know the temperature, but we like to use a thermometer.
- A slotted spoon or fry basket for retrieving the doughnuts from the hot oil.
- When the doughnuts come out of the oil, they need to sit on paper towels, which will absorb any excess oil.

Jelly-Filled Doughnuts (Sufganiyot)

The Jewish holiday of Hanukkah commemorates an ancient miracle in which the oil lamp in Jerusalem remained ablaze for eight days despite only having a meager amount of fuel. Every year, Jewish families celebrate the festival of lights by burning candles against the darkness of winter and eating oil-fried foods. Latkes (fried potato pancakes) might be more famous, but our favorite is *sufganiyot*, jelly doughnuts smothered in confectioners' sugar. Small and delightful, they are the perfect end to a long winter evening.

Makes twelve 3-inch doughnuts

  1½ pound (small cantaloupe-size portion) Brioche dough (page 65), Challah dough (page 147), or any other enriched dough in the book

  All-purpose flour, for dusting

  Vegetable oil, for frying

  2 cups Quick Raspberry Jam or other quick jam (page 351) or your favorite store-bought jam

  Confectioners' sugar, for dusting, or flavored sugar (1 cup sugar mixed with ½ teaspoon lemon zest or cinnamon.)

1. Follow the directions for the Honey-Glazed Doughnuts (page 202), roll the dough ½ inch thick, and don't cut a hole in the middle; just leave the circle of dough whole. Fry as directed.

2. Once the doughnuts are completely cool, poke the tip of a paring knife into one end to create a hole.

3. Fill a pastry bag, fitted with a large round pastry tip, with jam. Place the pastry tip in the doughnut and squeeze the jam into the center. You want enough jam so that every bite will have some, but not so much that it will explode when you eat it.

4. Dust with confectioners' sugar and serve.

Apple Fritters

These fried apple treats have been documented since at least medieval times, but they really took off during the American colonial period. Early British colonists grew thousands of varieties of apples, which quickly spread across the growing territories. All these apples were largely used to make cider—the hard stuff, as the water was unsafe to drink. Luckily for us, eating apples also caught on, and the fried fritter was a quick favorite. To this day we sing the praises of the apple fritter dipped in cinnamon sugar. What's not to love?

Makes 16 fritters

1½ pounds (small cantaloupe-size portion) Babka dough (page 173), Brioche dough (page 65), or any other enriched dough in the book

1 cup sugar

1 tablespoon ground cinnamon

All-purpose flour, for dusting

1 apple, cored, and chopped into ¼-inch cubes

Neutral-flavored oil, for frying, enough to fill a deep saucepan 3 inches from the top (see doughnut equipment sidebar, page 205)

1. Combine the sugar and cinnamon in a medium bowl, and set aside.

2. Dust the surface of the refrigerated dough with flour and cut off a 1½-pound (small cantaloupe–size) piece. Roll the dough out to a ½-inch-thick rectangle, about 8 × 10 inches.

3. Spread the apples over the dough and roll into a log. Coil the dough into a disk and knead the apples into the dough. Allow the dough to rest for 30 minutes.

4. Divide the dough in 24 pieces. (No need to roll them; they should be a bit shaggy.)

5. Heat the frying oil in a deep saucepan to 360°F to 370°F, as determined by a candy thermometer.

6. Drop the pieces of dough in the hot oil, three or four at a time, so that they have plenty of room to rise to the surface. Be careful not to overcrowd them, or they will not rise nicely.

7. After 1 minute, gently flip the fritters over with a slotted spoon and fry for another minute or so, until golden brown on both sides.

8. Remove the fritters from the oil, and place them on paper towels to drain the extra oil. While still warm, dredge them in the bowl of cinnamon sugar.

9. Repeat with the remaining dough until all the fritters are fried. Serve slightly warm.

Maple Long Johns

"There is no known history behind the name of these rectangular doughnuts stuffed with pastry cream and glazed with a sugar icing. When I was a kid, I thought they were named after the long underwear of the same name, but I can't find any evidence other than my 8-year-old logic. These doughnuts are like the love child of a Boston cream pie and an eclair. You can flavor the filling and the icing with anything, but being a Vermonter at heart, I grew up with the flavor of maple syrup and love it. I prefer grade B (now known as robust grade A syrup), because it has a deeper flavor and holds up to the pastry cream, but any maple syrup will do."—Zoë

Makes 6 long johns

- I pound (grapefruit-size portion) Brioche dough (page 65) or any other enriched dough from the book
- All-purpose flour, for dusting
- Neutral-flavored oil, for frying, enough to fill a deep saucepan 3 inches from the top (see doughnut equipment sidebar, page 205)
- I batch Pastry Cream (page 354)
- 2 tablespoons maple syrup

MAPLE GLAZE

- I cup confectioners' sugar
- 2 tablespoons maple syrup (or more as needed to create a thick, but pourable, glaze)
- ¼ teaspoon pure vanilla extract

½ cup coarsely chopped salted peanuts, for sprinkling on the doughnuts

1. Dust the surface of the refrigerated dough with flour and cut off a 1-pound (grapefruit-size) piece. Roll the dough out to a ¼-inch-thick rectangle, about 9 × 12 inches, and trim the edges. Cut the dough into 6 equal long rectangular pieces. Cover loosely with plastic wrap and allow to rest at room temperature for 20 minutes.

2. Heat the frying oil in a deep saucepan to 360°F to 370°F, as determined by a candy thermometer.

3. Fry the dough for 3 to 4 minutes, flipping to cook evenly, until golden.

4. Drain on paper towels and allow to cool completely before filling.

5. Mix the pastry cream with maple syrup. Poke a small hole on either end of each doughnut and fill with pastry cream using a pastry bag and a large, round tip.

6. Make the maple glaze: Whisk the sugar, maple syrup, and vanilla together in a bowl.

7. Dip the top of each doughnut in the glaze and sprinkle with salted peanuts. Enjoy.

Beignets

Beignets is French for fritters or, as we Americans like to call them, doughnuts. They're made from rich, yeasted dough; fried in oil; and then covered generously in confectioners' sugar. Here's a recreation, using our simple recipe, of the sweet confection made famous by Café Du Monde in New Orleans.

If the traditional beignets aren't decadent enough for you, try the chocolate or jam variation. They are quite simple to make, and when served with a fresh cup of *café au lait,* everyone becomes a little bit happier.

Makes about 6 beignets

I pound (grapefruit-size portion) Challah dough (page 147), Brioche dough (page 65), or any other enriched dough from the book

All-purpose flour, for dusting

Neutral-flavored oil for frying, enough to fill a deep saucepan 4 inches from the top (see doughnut equipment sidebar, page 205)

Confectioners' sugar, for dusting the beignets

1. Dust the surface of the refrigerated dough with flour and cut off a 1-pound (grapefruit-size) piece. Dust the piece with more flour and quickly shape it into a ball by stretching the surface of the dough around to the bottom, rotating the ball a quarter-turn as you go.

2. Roll the dough out to a ½-inch-thick rectangle, about 7 × 9 inches wide, on a lightly floured surface. Using a pizza cutter or knife, cut the dough into 2-inch squares. Cover loosely with plastic wrap and allow to rest at room temperature for 15 to 20 minutes.

3. Heat the frying oil in a deep saucepan to 360°F to 370°F, as determined by a candy thermometer.

4. Carefully drop the beignets in the hot oil, two or three at a time, so they have plenty of room to float to the surface. Do not overcrowd, or they will not rise nicely.

5. After 2 minutes, gently flip the beignets over with a slotted spoon and fry for another minute, or until golden brown on both sides.

6. Using the slotted spoon, remove the beignets from the oil and place them on paper towels to drain.

7. Repeat with the remaining dough until all the beignets are fried.

8. Dust generously with confectioners' sugar and enjoy.

VARIATION: CHOCOLATE- OR JAM-FILLED BEIGNETS

Makes about 6 beignets

1 pound (grapefruit-size portion) Challah dough (page 147) or Brioche dough (page 65)

4 ounces semisweet chocolate, cut into ½-ounce pieces, or 2 tablespoons of your favorite jam

Confectioners' sugar, for dusting the beignets

Follow the Beignets recipe, but roll the dough out to a ¼-inch-thick rectangle, about 9 × 12 inches, on a lightly floured surface. Using a pizza cutter or knife, cut the dough into 2-inch squares, then place ½ ounce of chocolate or a teaspoon of jam in the center of each square. Gather the edges of the dough around the filling, pinching at the center to form a seal. If you are not able to seal the edges *very* well, use a small amount of water to help stick them together. Cover loosely with plastic wrap and allow to rest at room temperature for 15 to 20 minutes. Fry, drain, and finish the beignets as directed. Serve slightly warm.

Ricotta-Stuffed Savory Doughnuts

We're not sure why doughnuts are typically sweet, not that we're complaining, but they are also delicious with savory fillings. *"When my family was in Naples, Italy, doing research for* Artisan Pizza and Flatbread in Five Minutes a Day, *we found a street stand that sold fried, stuffed doughnuts filled with fresh mozzarella and ricotta and served with tomato sauce. We found a way to pass this vendor on our way to everything."* —Zoë

Makes about 12 doughnuts

I pound (grapefruit-size piece) Olive Oil Dough (page 119), Challah dough (page 147), Super Strong Dough (page 59), or any dough from the book

All-purpose flour, for dusting

I cup shredded mozzarella

I cup whole-milk ricotta

¼ teaspoon freshly grated nutmeg

½ teaspoon dried oregano

Salt and freshly ground black pepper

Neutral-flavored oil, for frying, enough to fill a deep saucepan 4 inches from the top (see doughnut equipment sidebar, page 205)

Tomato sauce, for serving

1. Dust the surface of the refrigerated dough with flour and cut off a 1-pound (grapefruit-size) piece. Dust the piece with more flour and quickly shape it into a ball by stretching the surface of the dough around to the bottom, rotating the ball a quarter-turn as you go.

2. Roll the dough out to a ¼-inch-thick rectangle, about 9 × 12 inches on a lightly floured surface. Using a pizza cutter or knife, cut the dough into 2-inch squares.

3. Mix together the mozzarella, ricotta, nutmeg, oregano, salt, and pepper. Put about a tablespoon of the filling on each piece of dough, placing it so that you can easily close the dough around it. Brush the edge of the dough with water.

4. Press the dough closed around the filling, making sure that the dough is sealed well, so the filling won't come out while it is frying. Cover loosely with plastic wrap and allow to rest at room temperature for 15 to 20 minutes.

5. Heat the frying oil in a deep saucepan to 360°F to 370°F, as determined by a candy thermometer.

6. Carefully drop the stuffed doughnuts in the hot oil, two or three at a time, so they have plenty of room to rise to the surface. Do not overcrowd, or they will not rise nicely.

7. After 2 minutes, gently flip them over with a slotted spoon and fry for another minute or until golden brown on both sides.

8. Using the slotted spoon, remove the doughnuts from the oil and drain on paper towels. Repeat with the remaining dough until all are fried.

9. Serve with warm tomato sauce.

Fried Pita (Bhatoora)

This is a pillowy fried bread from the subcontinent of India. The dough is rolled incredibly thin and then fried in oil until it puffs, like a pita, into a soft, air-filled ball. We use our strong dough to get the best puff. If you fry just a little longer, the dough becomes cracker-like (see photo). Both versions are delicious with curries and dips.

The same dough can be pan-fried to make a *kulcha* (or stovetop naan). See the variation on page 220.

Makes 4 puffs

> 1 pound (grapefruit-size portion) Super Strong Dough (page 59)
>
> All-purpose flour, for dusting
>
> Neutral-flavored oil, for frying, enough to fill a deep saucepan 4 inches from the top (see doughnut equipment sidebar)

1. Dust the surface of the refrigerated dough with flour and cut off a 1-pound (grapefruit-size) piece. Divide the dough into 4 equal pieces, dust each one with more flour, and quickly shape it into a ball by stretching the surface of the dough around to the bottom, rotating the ball a quarter-turn as you go.

2. Fill a deep saucepan with at least 3 inches of oil and heat to 360°F to 370°F, as determined by a candy thermometer.

3. Roll each dough ball into a $\frac{1}{16}$-inch-thick circle, about 7 inches wide, on a lightly floured surface.

4. Carefully drop 1 dough circle into the hot oil. It will puff up and rise above the surface of the oil.

5. After 2 minutes, gently flip it over with a slotted spoon and fry for another 2 minutes or until golden brown on both sides. Fry longer for a crisp cracker. Using the slotted spoon, remove the fried dough from the oil and drain on paper towels.

6. Repeat with the remaining dough circles until all are fried. Serve warm.

VARIATION: KULCHA (PAN-FRIED NAAN)

We've had this bread in our past books and simply called it naan. It continues to be one of our all-time favorites, since it is so simple and quick to make, and who doesn't like a dough pan-fried in butter or ghee? To make your own clarified butter or ghee, which has a nutty taste and can be cooked to higher temperatures than butter without burning, see page 12.

Makes 1 flatbread

> ¼ pound (peach-size portion) White Bread Master Recipe dough (page 48), Light Whole
> Wheat Bread dough (page 77), or Semolina Bread dough (page 89)
> All-purpose flour, for dusting
> 1 tablespoon ghee, butter, or oil
> Unsalted butter, for brushing the loaf (if ghee is unavailable)

1. Dust the surface of the refrigerated dough with flour and cut off a ¼-pound (peach-size) piece. Dust the piece with more flour and quickly shape it into a ball by stretching the surface of the dough around to the bottom, rotating the ball a quarter-turn as you go. Using your hands and a rolling pin, and minimal flour, roll the dough out into a ⅛-inch-thick round, 8 to 9 inches wide.

2. Heat a heavy 12-inch cast-iron skillet over high heat. When water droplets flicked into the pan skitter across the surface and evaporate quickly, the pan is ready. Add the ghee.

3. Drop the rolled dough round into the skillet, decrease the heat to medium, and cover the skillet to trap the steam and heat.

4. Check for doneness with a spatula at about 3 minutes, or sooner if the kulcha smells like it's browning too quickly. Adjust the heat as needed. Flip the naan when the underside is richly browned.

5. Continue cooking for another 2 to 6 minutes, or until the kulcha feels firm, even at the edges, and the second side is browned. If you've rolled a thicker kulcha, or if you're using dough with whole grains, you'll need more pan time.

6. Remove the bread from the pan, brush with butter if the dough was cooked in oil, and serve.

12

CHRISTMAS BREADS

Modern Christmas celebrations—with an ornamented tree, family festivities, gifts, and feasts—have only been around since the nineteenth century. Traditions dating back to the ninth century and the reign of Holy Roman Emperor Charlemagne were a bit more raucous. Dickens's 1843 novel *A Christmas Carol* is thought by some historians to have spurred a reinvention of holiday observance—it's a story of redemption and charity that unites people across social divisions. Christmas is generally celebrated on December 25th, although the ubiquitous Christmas music starts at Thanksgiving. The way the holiday is celebrated varies widely depending on the country and even the region, but many cultures that celebrate Christmas include a special bread that's baked only during this time of year. In this chapter, we'll highlight some of the unique bread traditions from the many cultures in Europe and beyond that celebrate this day.

Panettone

Panettone is one of the most popular Christmas breads sold all over Italy (and the United States) during the holidays. It originated in Milan around the fifteenth century and has been the subject of much lore. A commonly told story of how this bejeweled bread came to be goes something like this: A young nobleman falls in love with a baker's daughter named Toni. He disguises himself as a pastry chef's apprentice and creates the tall, fruit-studded bread to present to Toni, calling it *"Pan de Toni."* The bread is a success in the bakery, and the father blesses the marriage.

The story is as rich and fanciful as the bread, made with dried fruit and the essence of lemons and vanilla. There are traditional panettone molds that are very high-sided and come either straight or fluted. They can be found at cooking stores or on the Web. You can use a brioche mold, but the bread won't have the classic high sides. Paper panettone molds are available from baking supply stores, or you can use smaller tulip liners (found on Amazon) and bake them in muffin tins (see book cover).

Makes at least three loaves slightly larger than 1½ pounds each. The recipe is easily doubled or halved.

INGREDIENT	VOLUME (U.S.)	WEIGHT (U.S.)	WEIGHT (METRIC)
Lukewarm water (100°F or below)	1½ cups	12 ounces	340 grams
Granulated yeast[1]	1 tablespoon	0.35 ounce	10 grams
Kosher salt[1]	1 tablespoon	0.6 ounce	17 grams
Honey	½ cup	6 ounces	170 grams
Large eggs, lightly beaten	8	1 pound	455 grams
Unsalted butter, melted and slightly cooled	1 cup (2 sticks)	8 ounces	225 grams
Lemon extract	1 teaspoon		
Pure vanilla extract	2 teaspoons		

Lemon zest, grated	2 teaspoons		
Mixed dried and/or candied fruit[2]	2 cups	12 ounces	340 grams
All-purpose flour	7½ cups	2 pounds, 5½ ounces	1,065 grams
Egg wash (1 egg beaten with 1 tablespoon water), for brushing the loaf			
Sugar, for sprinkling on the loaf			

[1]Can decrease (see pages 15 and 33).

[2] Golden raisins, dried pineapple, dried apricots, dried cherries, and candied citrus peel are a few fruits that we've tried and loved in this bread.

1. Mixing and storing the dough: Mix the water, yeast, salt, honey, eggs, melted butter, extracts, and lemon zest in a 6-quart bowl or a lidded (not airtight) food container.

2. Mix in the dried fruit and flour without kneading, using a heavy-duty stand mixer (with paddle), a Danish dough whisk, or a spoon. If you're not using a machine, you may need to use wet hands to incorporate the last bit of flour. The dough will be loose, but will firm up when chilled (don't try to use it without chilling).

3. Cover (not airtight) and allow to rest at room temperature until the dough rises for 2 hours.

4. The dough can be used as soon as it's chilled after the initial rise, or frozen for later use. Refrigerate the container and use over the next 5 days. To freeze dough see page 42.

5. On baking day, dust the surface of the refrigerated dough with flour and cut off a 1½-pound (small cantaloupe-size) piece. Dust the piece with more flour and quickly shape it into a ball by stretching the surface of the dough around to the bottom, rotating the ball a quarter-turn as you go. Place the ball in the paper panettone mold, seam side down.

6. Cover loosely with plastic wrap and allow to rest at room temperature for 90 minutes.

7. Preheat the oven to 350°F, with a rack placed in the center of the oven.

8. Brush the panettone with egg wash. Bake for 50 to 55 minutes, or until golden brown and hollow-sounding when tapped. The amount of dough and baking times will vary depending on the panettone mold size.

9. Allow to cool on a rack before serving.

VARIATION: PANETTONE MUFFINS

Makes 6 muffins

Follow the Panettone recipe but divide the 1½-pounds of dough into 6 equal pieces. Form them into balls and let them rest in muffin cup liners. (The ones we used are called tulip liners.) Cover and allow to rest for 45 minutes. Brush with egg wash. Bake at 350°F for 30 to 35 minutes, or until golden and set.

Bohemian Raisin Braid (Vánočka)

Vánočka (pronounced van-ooch-ka) is a Christmas bread made in the Czech Republic and is very similar to challah and brioche, but is often stuffed full of raisins and flavored with booze. The dough is identical to *mazanec*, which is served at Easter. According to superstition, when making this bread at Christmas, you should jump up and down three times while the dough rises and think good things about the people you love. Who knows if it works to help the bread turn out well, but it sounds like a great tradition, so we highly recommend it.

Makes I braid

I pound (grapefruit-size portion) Easter Raisin Bread dough (page 285)

All-purpose flour, for dusting

Egg yolk glaze (I egg yolk beaten with I tablespoon milk), for brushing the loaf

ICING

I cup confectioners' sugar

I tablespoon milk

¼ teaspoon almond extract

½ cup whole pecans, toasted, for decorating the loaf

12 candied cherries, for decorating the loaf (optional)

1. To bake: Line a baking sheet with parchment paper or a silicone mat. Dust the surface of the refrigerated dough with flour and cut off a 1-pound (grapefruit-size) piece. Divide the dough into 3 equal pieces. Dust each piece with more flour and quickly shape into a ball by stretching the surface of the dough around to the bottom, rotating the ball a quarter-turn as you go.

2. Gently roll and stretch each dough ball, dusting with flour so your hands don't stick

Visit BreadIn5.com, where you'll find recipes, photos, videos, and instructional material.

227

to it, until you have a long rope, about ¾ inch thick, with tapered ends. You may need to let the dough relax for 5 minutes so it won't resist your efforts.

3. Braid the loaf: See Challah (page 147) for instructions.

4. Cover loosely with plastic wrap and allow to rest at room temperature for 90 minutes.

5. Preheat the oven to 350°F, with a rack placed in the center of the oven.

6. Brush the loaf with egg yolk glaze.

7. Bake for about 30 minutes. The challah is done when golden brown and the braid near the center of the loaf is set.

8. Make the icing: While the braid is cooling, mix all the icing ingredients together in a small bowl. Drizzle the icing over the cooled bread and decorate with the pecans and cherries (if using).

VARIATION: HOUSKA
(FRUIT-STUDDED BRAID TOWER)

Houska is a braided bread from the Czech Republic that seems to be served both at Christmas and Easter, depending on the household. We've seen it braided and shaped in many ways; like challah, it can be round, multi-stranded, or stacked.

1¾ pounds Easter Raisin Bread dough (page 285)

Egg wash (1 egg beaten with 1 tablespoon water), for brushing the loaf

½ cup toasted sliced almonds, for sprinkling on the loaf

2 tablespoons raw sugar, for sprinkling on the loaf

Braid the dough as done in the Stacked Challah Braids with a Twist (page 163). Brush the dough with the egg wash, then sprinkle with the toasted sliced almonds and raw sugar. Follow the baking instructions for the Stacked Challah Braids.

VARIATION: OSTERZOPF
(BRAIDED GERMAN WREATH)

Just after dusk on a German Easter Sunday, you might find entire communities coming together to throw their old Christmas trees into a bonfire. The fire symbolizes an end to the darkness of winter. The bonfire usually turns into a big party, which can last all night until the morning of Easter Monday. The *osterzopf,* usually shaped into a braided wreath, might be decorated with almonds and raisins or other dried fruit. It would be the perfect hearty snack after a night of tending the bonfire.

Follow the recipe for Bohemian Raisin Bread and after forming the braid, stretch it out and then join the two ends. Rest, bake and, decorate as directed.

Stollen

There is a large German population in Minnesota, and when our first book came out, a reader asked how to convert his grandmother's stollen recipe to our five-minute method. We did just that and included a whole-grain version in **_Healthy Bread in Five Minutes a Day,_** but here is a recipe for Christmas that's more indulgent (and probably even closer to what grandma made). The bread's shape is thought to resemble the baby Jesus's swaddling clothes. After the loaf comes out of the oven, you dust it with confectioners' sugar for extra sweetness—and it reminds us of a wintry blanket of snow. Stollen comes from the German city of Dresden, and the recipe dates back to at least the fifteenth century. To this day, Dresden celebrates its annual Stollenfest during Advent. This outdoor parade features an enormous stollen, which is large enough to be shared by thousands of attendees. Now that must be some oven! We assume you'll want something a bit smaller, but you are welcome to bake all of this dough in one giant loaf.

**Makes at least three loaves slightly larger than 1½ pounds each. The recipe is easily doubled or halved.**

INGREDIENT	VOLUME (U.S.)	WEIGHT (U.S.)	WEIGHT (METRIC)
Lukewarm water (100°F or below)	1½ cups	12 ounces	340 grams
Granulated yeast[1]	1 tablespoon	0.35 ounce	10 grams
Kosher salt[1]	1 tablespoon	0.6 ounce	17 grams
Sugar	½ cup	4 ounces	115 grams
Large eggs, lightly beaten	2	4 ounces	115 grams
Vegetable oil	½ cup	3.5 ounces	100 grams
Brandy	¼ cup	2 ounces	55 grams
Pure vanilla extract	2 teaspoons		
All-purpose flour	6½ cups	2 pounds	910 grams

(Continued)			
Ground cardamom	½ teaspoon		
Mixed dried and/or candied fruit[2]	1½ cups	9 ounces	255 grams
Almond paste	½ cup per loaf	4 ounces	115 grams
Egg wash (1 egg beaten with 1 tablespoon water), for brushing the loaf			
Confectioners' sugar, for dusting the loaf			

[1]Can decrease (see pages 15 and 33).

[2] Golden raisins, dried pineapple, dried apricots, dried cherries, and candied citrus peel are a few fruits that we've tried and loved in this bread.

1. Mixing and storing the dough: Mix the water, yeast, salt, sugar, eggs, oil, brandy, and vanilla in a 6-quart bowl or a lidded (not airtight) food container.

2. Mix in the flour, cardamom, and dried fruit without kneading, using a heavy-duty stand mixer (with paddle), a Danish dough whisk, or a spoon. If you're not using a machine, you may need to use wet hands to incorporate the last bit of flour. The dough will be loose but will firm up when chilled (don't try to use it without chilling).

3. Cover (not airtight) and allow to rest at room temperature until the dough rises for 2 hours.

4. The dough can be used as soon as it's chilled after the initial rise, or frozen for later use. Refrigerate the container and use over the next 5 days. To freeze dough see page 42.

5. On baking day, dust the surface of the refrigerated dough with flour and cut off a 1½-pound (small cantaloupe-size) piece. Dust the piece with more flour and quickly shape it into a ball by stretching the surface of the dough around to the bottom, rotating the ball a quarter-turn as you go.

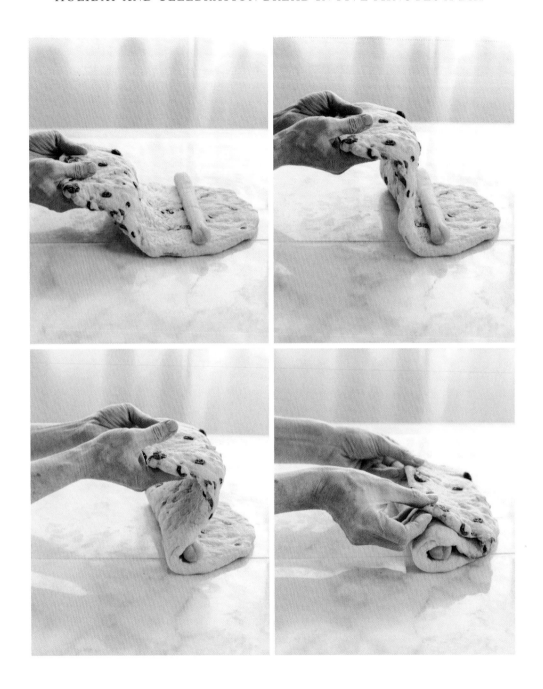

6. Using a rolling pin, roll the dough out to a ¼-inch-thick oval. As you roll the dough, use enough flour to prevent the dough from sticking to the work surface, but not so much as to make it dry.

7. Mold the almond paste into a log and place across the short end of the dough about one-third of the way from the end. Lift and fold the remaining two-thirds of dough to form an S-shape over the almond filling. The end of the dough will lie near the middle of the top of the loaf. Place on a parchment paper–lined baking sheet. Cover loosely with plastic wrap and allow to rest at room temperature for 90 minutes.

8. Preheat the oven to 350°F, with a rack placed in the center of the oven.

9. Remove the plastic wrap and brush the stollen with egg wash. Bake in the center of the oven for 35 to 40 minutes, or until golden brown.

10. Allow to cool, and then dust generously with confectioners' sugar and serve.

Julekage

Julekage or *Julebrød*, which literally means "Yule bread" in Norwegian, can be traced back to pagan times. In late autumn, a loaf of bread was baked using the last scraps of harvest, and then it was stored inside during winter. It gained associations with Christmas because it spent the season decorating the home. When spring finally arrived, the stale bread was taken out and shared among the workers and their horses, and then the crumbs, which supposedly had powers of fertility, were mixed in with the new seeds to be planted. Nowadays, this raisin bread is meant to be eaten fresh, preferably with butter and Quick Raspberry Jam (page 351).

Yield 1 round loaf

1½ pounds (small cantaloupe-size portion) Stollen dough (page 231), Easter Raisin Bread dough (page 285), or any other enriched dough in the book, with ¾ cup raisins kneaded into it

All-purpose flour, for dusting

Egg yolk glaze (1 egg yolk beaten with 1 tablespoon milk and a pinch salt), for brushing the loaf

ICING

1½ teaspoons milk

¼ cup confectioners' sugar

¼ teaspoon pure almond extract

¼ cup slivered or sliced almonds, toasted, for sprinkling on the loaf (optional)

1. To bake: Dust the surface of the refrigerated dough with flour and cut off a 1½-pound (small cantaloupe-size) piece. Dust the piece with more flour and quickly shape it into a ball by stretching the surface of the dough around to the bottom, rotating the ball a quarter-turn as you go.

2. Place the dough ball on a baking sheet lined with parchment paper. Cover loosely with plastic wrap and allow to rest at room temperature for 90 minutes.

3. Preheat the oven to 350°F, with a rack placed in the center of the oven.

4. Brush the loaf with egg glaze. Bake for about 35 minutes, or until golden brown. Allow to cool on a wire rack.

5. Make the icing: While the bread cools, whisk together the milk, sugar, and almond extract.

6. When the Julekage is cooled, spoon the icing on the top, and sprinkle with the almonds (if using). Allow to cool before serving.

Limpa

This is the traditional Swedish sweet rye bread served at the holidays. Honey and orange zest mingle with the more exotic flavors of anise and cardamom to make a flavorful and fragrant treat.

Makes four 1-pound loaves. The recipe is easily doubled or halved.

INGREDIENT	VOLUME (U.S.)	WEIGHT (U.S.)	WEIGHT (METRIC)
Lukewarm water (100°F or below)	3 cups	1 pound, 8 ounces	680 grams
Granulated yeast[1]	1 tablespoon	0.35 ounce	10 grams
Kosher salt[1]	1 tablespoon	0.6 ounce	17 grams
Honey	½ cup	6 ounces	170 grams
Aniseed, ground	½ teaspoon		
Cardamom, ground	1 teaspoon		
Orange zest, grated	1½ teaspoons		
Rye flour	1 cup	4¼ ounces	120 grams
All-purpose flour	5½ cups	1 pound, 11½ ounces	780 grams
Egg wash (1 egg beaten with 1 tablespoon water), for brushing the loaf			
Spiced sugar for the top of each loaf: ¼ cup confectioners' sugar mixed with ¼ teaspoon ground aniseed			

[1]Can decrease (see pages 15 and 33).

1. Mixing and storing the dough: Mix the water, yeast, salt, honey, aniseed, cardamom, and orange zest in a 6-quart bowl or a lidded (not airtight) food container.

2. Mix in the flours without kneading, using a heavy-duty stand mixer (with paddle), a Danish dough whisk, or a spoon. If you're not using a machine, you may need to use wet hands to incorporate the last bit of flour.

3. Cover (not airtight) and allow to rest at room temperature until the dough rises for 2 hours.

4. The dough can be used immediately after the initial rise, though it is easier to handle when cold. Refrigerate the container and use over the next 7 days.

5. On baking day, grease an 8-inch cake pan. Dust the surface of the refrigerated dough with flour and cut off a 1-pound (grapefruit-size) piece. Dust the piece with more flour and quickly shape it into a ball by stretching the surface of the dough around to the bottom, rotating the ball a quarter-turn as you go. Drop the dough into the prepared pan, cover loosely with plastic wrap, and allow to rest at room temperature for 60 minutes.

6. Preheat the oven to 375°F, with a rack placed in the center of the oven.

7. Before baking, brush with egg wash and slash the dough in a decorative pattern.

8. Bake for 35 to 40 minutes, or until golden brown and firm.

9. Allow to cool on a rack before dusting with the spiced confectioners' sugar.

Swedish Tea Ring

This is like an ultrafancy cinnamon roll baked as a wreath and served at Christmas time in Sweden. The cuts and twists of the dough make for a super-festive bread that is actually really easy to make, so don't leave this one for just once a year.

Makes 1 ring; serves 12

3 tablespoons unsalted butter, melted

¼ cup sugar

1 tablespoon ground cinnamon

Pinch salt

1½ pounds (small cantaloupe-size) piece Stollen dough (page 231), Brioche dough
    (page 65), or any other enriched dough in the book

All-purpose flour, for dusting

Egg wash (1 egg beaten with 1 tablespoon water), for brushing the loaf

ICING

1 cup confectioners' sugar

¼ teaspoon almond extract

1 tablespoon milk (or more to get the icing to drizzle)

½ cup sliced almonds, toasted, for sprinkling on the loaf (optional)

1. Line a baking sheet with parchment paper or a silicone mat.

2. In a small bowl, combine the melted butter, sugar, cinnamon, and salt.

3. Dust the surface of the refrigerated dough with flour and quickly shape it into a rough ball by stretching the surface of the dough around to the bottom, rotating the ball a quarter-turn as you go.

Visit BreadIn5.com, where you'll find recipes, photos, videos, and instructional material.

243

4. Using a rolling pin, roll the dough out to a ⅛-inch-thick rectangle, about 14 × 18 inches. As you roll out the dough, add flour as needed to prevent sticking.

5. Spread the butter mixture evenly over the dough.

6. Starting with the long side of the dough, roll it up into a log. Pinch the seam closed. Stretch the log until it is about 1½ inches thick. Join the 2 ends together to form a wreath shape; pinch together to seal. Place on the prepared baking sheet. Stretch the dough to make sure you have a nice, wide opening in the middle of your wreath, but leave plenty of room around the edge.

7. Cover loosely with plastic wrap and allow to rest at room temperature for 40 minutes.

8. Preheat the oven to 350°F, with a rack placed in the center of the oven.

9. Brush lightly with egg wash. Make evenly spaced cuts all the way around the wreath about 1 inch apart. The cuts should go just about to the bottom of the ring, but not quite to the bottom.

10. Gently pull every other piece to the outside of the ring and then twist that piece to face up. Do the same with the remaining pieces, but have them face up on the inside of the ring. The ones on the inside of the ring may not lay flat on the baking sheet, which is fine.

11. Bake for 35 to 40 minutes, or until golden brown and well set.

12. Allow to cool for about 20 minutes.

13. Make the icing: In a small bowl, mix together the confectioners' sugar, almond extract, and milk until smooth. Drizzle the icing over the top and sprinkle with the almonds (if using). Serve warm or cool.

Finnish Pulla

Pulla's mild fragrance comes from a mixture of cardamom, vanilla, and walnuts. Native to Finland, pulla is a braided bread with a soft, airy interior and a shiny brown exterior. You can expect to be served a slice of pulla with your afternoon coffee in any Finnish household. Coffee culture is very important in Finland; almost everyone drinks coffee all day long, usually accompanied by pulla or another sweet bread. As the days get shorter and snow begins to fall, pulla's comforting cardamom flavor is a perfect pick-me-up on a dark winter afternoon.

Makes two 1½-pound loaves. The recipe is easily doubled or halved.

INGREDIENT	VOLUME (U.S.)	WEIGHT (U.S.)	WEIGHT (METRIC)
Whole milk	2½ cups	1 pound, 4 ounces	570 grams
Large eggs	3	6 ounces	170 grams
Pure vanilla extract	1 tablespoon		
Granulated yeast[1]	1 tablespoon	0.35 ounce	10 grams
Kosher salt[1]	1 tablespoon	0.6 ounce	17 grams
Sugar	⅓ cup	2¼ ounces	65 grams
All-purpose flour	6¼ cups	1 pound, 15 ounces	880 grams
Potato flour	¼ cup	1¾ ounces	50 grams
Ground cardamom	2 teaspoons		
Walnuts, chopped	1½ cups	5½ ounces	155 grams
Unsalted butter	8 tablespoons (1 stick)	4 ounces	113 grams
Egg wash (1 egg beaten with 1 tablespoon water)			
Raw sugar, for sprinkling on the loaf			

[1]Can decrease (see pages 15 and 33).

ICING

½ cup confectioners' sugar

2 tablespoons heavy cream

1 drop almond extract

Walnut halves, for decorating the top

1. Mixing and storing the dough: Mix the milk, yeast, salt, and sugar in a 5-quart bowl or a lidded (not airtight) food container.

2. In a small bowl, whisk together the all-purpose flour with the potato flour. Mix in the flours and butter with the milk mixture without kneading, using a heavy-duty stand mixer (with paddle), a Danish dough whisk, or a spoon.

3. Cover (not airtight) and allow to rest at room temperature until the dough rises for 2 hours.

4. The dough can be used as soon as it's thoroughly chilled, at least 3 hours. Refrigerate the container and use over the next 5 days. To freeze dough, see page 42.

5. On baking day, dust the surface of the refrigerated dough with flour and cut off a 1½-pound (small cantaloupe-size) piece. Divide the dough into 3 smaller balls. Roll and stretch each ball into a ¾-inch-thick rope about 18 inches long and taper the ends. Form a braid (see page 147) on a baking sheet lined with parchment paper.

6. Pinch one end together and braid the ropes, pinching the other end together when you're done.

7. Cover loosely with plastic wrap and allow to rest at room temperature for 90 minutes.

8. Preheat the oven to 350°F, with a rack placed in the center of the oven.

9. Just before baking, brush the top crust with egg wash. Sprinkle with raw sugar (or you can substitute regular granulated white sugar).

10. Bake for about 40 minutes, or until golden brown. Cool on a wire rack.

11. Make the icing: Mix together the confectioners' sugar, cream, and almond extract.

12. Allow the bread to cool before drizzling with icing, and then scatter walnut halves over the top.

VARIATION: PULLA WREATH

Follow the recipe for Finnish Pulla and after forming the braid, stretch it slightly and shape into a circle, pinching the 2 ends together. Cover, allow to rest, and bake as directed.

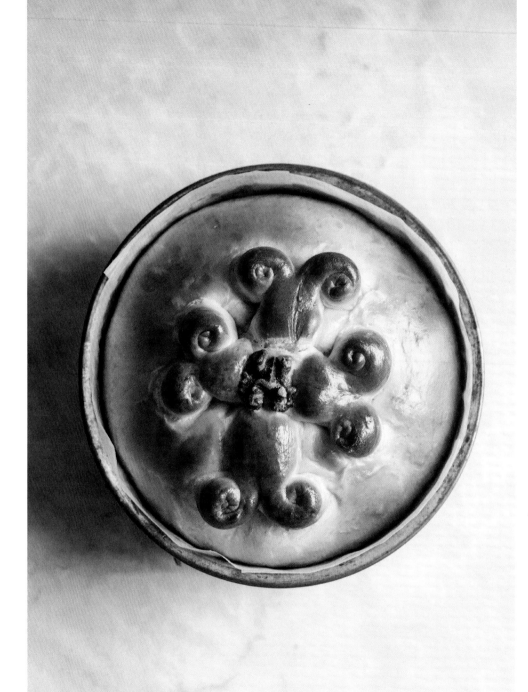

Greek Cross-Topped Bread (Christopsomo)

No Greek Christmas would be complete without a loaf of orange-scented *christopsomo*. This bread is crowned with coils of dough in the shape of a cross. Traditionally, families would decorate the top of the bread with other symbols as well, personalized to their goals and professions. For example, newlyweds might like a christopsomo decorated with dough in the shape of interlaced wedding rings, while farmers would prefer images of crops and livestock. When you create your christopsomo, think about your own hopes for the coming year! For extra authenticity, serve this bread with figs for prosperity and honey for sweetness.

Makes 1 loaf

1 pound (grapefruit-size portion) Challah dough (page 147), Brioche dough (page 65), or any other enriched dough in the book

All-purpose flour, for dusting

1 tablespoon grated orange zest

Egg yolk glaze (1 egg yolk beaten with 1 tablespoon milk), for brushing the loaf

1 walnut half, for decorating the loaf

1. To bake: Grease an 8-inch cake pan and line with parchment paper.

2. Dust the surface of the refrigerated dough with flour and cut off a 1-pound (grapefruit-size) piece. Using a rolling pin, roll the dough out to a ¼-inch-thick rectangle, about 9 × 12 inches. Spread the orange zest over the dough. Roll the dough up into a log and then form it into a ball. Knead the ball for several minutes to distribute the orange zest throughout the dough.

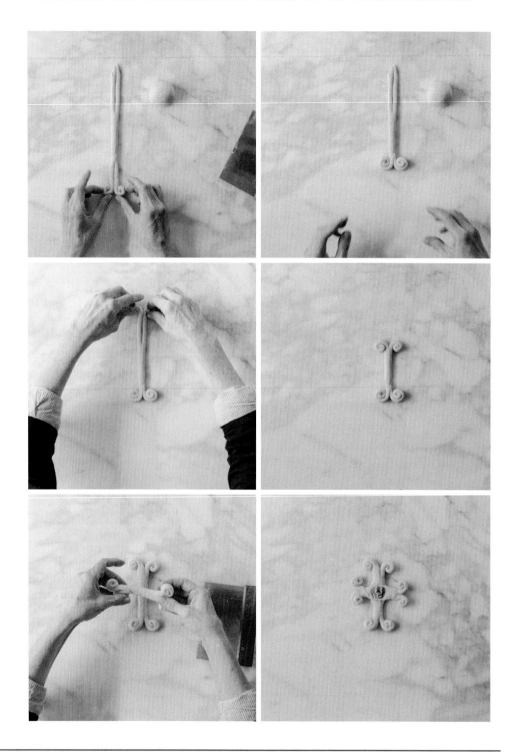

3. Pinch off 2 small pieces the size of plums. Dust the pieces with more flour and quickly shape it into balls by stretching the surface of the dough around to the bottom, rotating the ball a quarter-turn as you go.

4. Place the large ball of dough in the prepared pan. Stretch the smaller balls into long ropes, about 12 inches long. Cut a 4-inch slash on each end. Cross the 2 strands of dough over the resting ball of dough to form a cross on the top of the loaf. Curl each cut end piece into a coil to hold the walnuts. Brush with the egg glaze, press the walnuts into the coils, cover loosely with plastic wrap, and allow to rest at room temperature for 60 minutes.

5. Preheat the oven to 350°F, with a rack placed in the center of the oven.

6. Before baking, brush with the egg again.

7. Bake for 35 to 40 minutes, or until golden brown and firm.

8. Allow to cool on a rack before serving.

Chestnut Chocolate Bread

"There is nothing more Christmas-y than chestnuts, and they pair with chocolate like magic. This bread is not traditional to any specific culture; we just loved it! So it is now a tradition in my home."—Zoë

Makes one 2-pound tall bread

2 pounds (cantaloupe-size piece) Challah dough (page 147), Brioche dough (page 65), or any other enriched dough in the book

All-purpose flour, for dusting

1 cup chopped roasted chestnuts

1 cup finely chopped chocolate

Egg yolk glaze (1 egg yolk beaten with 1 tablespoon milk), for brushing the loaf

1. To bake: Generously grease a panettone mold (page 27).

2. Dust the surface of the refrigerated dough with flour and cut off a 2-pound (cantaloupe-size) piece. Using a rolling pin, roll the dough out to a ¼-inch-thick rectangle. Spread the chestnuts and chocolate over the dough. Roll the dough up into a log and then form it into a ball. Knead the ball for several minutes to distribute the chestnuts and chocolate throughout the dough.

3. Dust the dough with more flour and quickly shape it into a ball by stretching the surface of the dough around to the bottom, rotating the ball a quarter-turn as you go.

4. Place the large ball of dough in the prepared pan. Cover loosely with plastic wrap and allow to rest at room temperature for 90 minutes.

5. Preheat the oven to 350°F, with a rack placed in the center of the oven.

6. Before baking, brush with the egg yolk glaze.

7. Bake for about 50 minutes, or until deep brown and firm. Smaller or larger loaves will require adjustments in baking time.

8. Remove from pan and allow to cool on a rack before serving.

Kugelhopf

The *kugelhopf* can be found all over central Europe, from eastern France to Austria, during the holidays and the spelling can vary widely from country to country. Variations include *gugelhupf* and *kouglof,* but they all refer to a tall, Bundt-shaped brioche. The kugelhopf is most iconic of Austrian culture, where it is often decorated with elegant grooved swirls and studded with almonds. The loaves are sold in any coffeehouse in Vienna and are perfect for a refined afternoon tea or a relaxed family brunch. This dough is also delightful "baked" in a waffle iron for a fun Sunday brunch (see page 260).

Makes enough dough for at least three 1½-pound loaves. The recipe is easily doubled or halved.

INGREDIENT	VOLUME (U.S.)	WEIGHT (U.S.)	WEIGHT (METRIC)
Whole milk, warmed (100°F or below)	2 cups	1 pound	455 grams
Granulated yeast[1]	1 tablespoon	0.35 ounce	10 grams
Kosher salt[1]	1 tablespoon	0.6 ounce	17 grams
Sugar, plus more for the pan	1 cup	7 ounces	200 grams
Large eggs, lightly beaten	4	8 ounces	225 grams
Egg yolks	4	4 ounces	115 grams
Lemon zest, grated	1½ tablespoons		
Rum or orange juice	½ cup	4 ounces	115 grams
Raisins	1½ cups	7 ounces	200 grams
All-purpose flour	6⅔ cups	2 pounds, 1 ounce	945 grams
Unsalted butter, melted, plus more for greasing the pan	1½ cups (3 sticks)	12 ounces	340 grams
Sliced almonds	3 tablespoons		

[1]Can decrease (see pages 15 and 33).

1. Mixing and storing the dough: Mix the milk, yeast, salt, sugar, eggs, yolks, 1 tablespoon of the lemon zest, the raisins, and ¼ cup of the rum (if using) in a 5-quart bowl or a lidded (not airtight) food container.

2. Mix in the flour and butter with the milk mixture without kneading, using a heavy-duty stand mixer (with paddle), a Danish dough whisk, or a spoon.

3. Cover (not airtight), and allow to rest at room temperature for 2 hours, and then refrigerate.

4. The dough can be used as soon as it's thoroughly chilled, at least 3 hours. Refrigerate the container and use over the next 3 days. To freeze dough, see page 42.

5. On baking day, grease a nonstick kugelhopf pan generously with butter. Dust with sugar and sprinkle almonds on the bottom of the pan. Dust the surface of the refrigerated dough with flour and cut off a 1½-pound (small cantaloupe-size) piece. Dust with more flour and quickly shape it into a ball by stretching the surface of the dough around to the bottom, rotating the ball a quarter-turn as you go. Elongate the ball into an oval and place the loaf pan.

6. Cover loosely with plastic wrap and allow to rest at room temperature for 90 minutes.

7. Preheat the oven to 350°F, with a rack placed in the center of the oven.

8. Bake for about 40 minutes, or until the loaf is browned and firm.

9. While the cake is baking make the glaze: Combine ¼ cup water, ¼ cup sugar, the remaining ¼ cup rum (or you can use orange juice), and the remaining ½ tablespoon lemon zest in a small pan and simmer until the sugar is melted.

10. When the cake comes out of the oven, poke the bottom multiple times (25 to 30 times) with a skewer; brush the cake with half the glaze. Allow to cool for 10 minutes.

11. Invert the cake onto a serving plate and brush with the remaining glaze, avoiding the almonds. Allow to cool completely before serving.

VARIATION: KUGELHOPF WAFFLES

Roll out a small amount of dough (about 6 ounces) and place it in your waffle iron and cook according to the manufacturer's instructions. Slather with butter and maple syrup and whipped cream and quick jam (page 351) and whatever else you can think of. It's a party on a plate. Zoë's kids prefer this made without the raisins and with chocolate chips instead, so you can play with the additions your family will enjoy.

Saint Lucia Saffron Buns

December 13th is Saint Lucia Day in Sweden, where these saffron-scented, S-shaped buns are a pre-Christmas tradition that reflects Scandinavia's long history in the global spice trade. Saffron is a spice that comes from the flower of a very particular crocus. Tradition holds that Lucia, a Sicilian saint, made her way to Scandinavia to spread the faith, and with her came warming spices, like saffron, cinnamon, and cardamom. No one is really sure why saffron became associated with Lucia, but her name means "light," and we think these bright yellow buns were a warm comfort when the daylight hours become short in the winter. Also, try Sheermal, a Persian flatbread made with the same dough (page 129).

Makes 32 buns

INGREDIENT	VOLUME (U.S.)	WEIGHT (U.S.)	WEIGHT (METRIC)
Water	½ cup	4 ounces	115 grams
Saffron threads	½ teaspoon		
Whole milk	1½ cups	12 ounces	346 grams
Quark[1]	½ cup	4 ounces	120 grams
Eggs	3	6 ounces	170 grams
Granulated yeast[2]	1 tablespoon	0.35 ounce	10 grams
Kosher salt[2]	1 tablespoon	0.6 ounce	17 grams
Sugar	⅓ cup	2¼ ounces	65 grams
Ground cardamom	½ teaspoon		
Bread flour	6¼ cups	1 pound, 15 ounces	880 grams
Potato flour	¼ cup	1¾ ounces	50 grams
Unsalted butter, melted	8 tablespoons (1 stick)	4 ounces	115 grams

(Continued)	
Egg white wash (1 egg white beaten with 1 teaspoon water), for brushing the buns	
Pearl sugar, for sprinkling on the buns	
Golden raisins, for decorating the buns	16

¹See page 11 for substitutions.

²Can decrease (see page 15 and 33).

1. Mixing and storing the dough: Mix the water, saffron threads, milk, quark, eggs, yeast, salt, sugar, and cardamom in a 5-quart bowl or a lidded (not airtight) food container.

2. In a small bowl, whisk together the all-purpose flour with the potato flour. Mix in the flours and butter with the saffron mixture without kneading, using a heavy-duty stand mixer (with paddle), a Danish dough whisk, or a spoon.

3. Cover (not airtight), allow to rest at room temperature for 2 hours, and then refrigerate.

4. The dough can be used as soon as it's thoroughly chilled, at least 3 hours. Refrigerate the container and use over the next 5 days. To freeze dough, see page 42.

5. On baking day, line a baking sheet with parchment paper. Dust the surface of the refrigerated dough with flour and cut off a 1-pound (grapefruit-size) piece. Divide that piece into 8 equal pieces. Dust each piece with more flour and quickly shape them into balls by stretching the surface of the dough around to the bottom, rotating the ball a quarter-turn as you go.

6. Elongate the balls of dough into 20-inch ropes. Working with 1 rope at a time, starting at 1 end, coil the dough into the middle. Coil the other end into the middle, creating an S-shape. Place on the baking sheet.

7. Cover loosely with plastic wrap and allow to rest at room temperature for 40 minutes.

8. Preheat the oven to 350°F, with a rack placed in the center of the oven.

9. Brush the buns with the egg white wash. Sprinkle with the pearl sugar and press a golden raisin into the center of each coiled section.

10. Bake for 25 minutes, or until the buns are golden brown.

11. Allow to cool on a rack before serving.

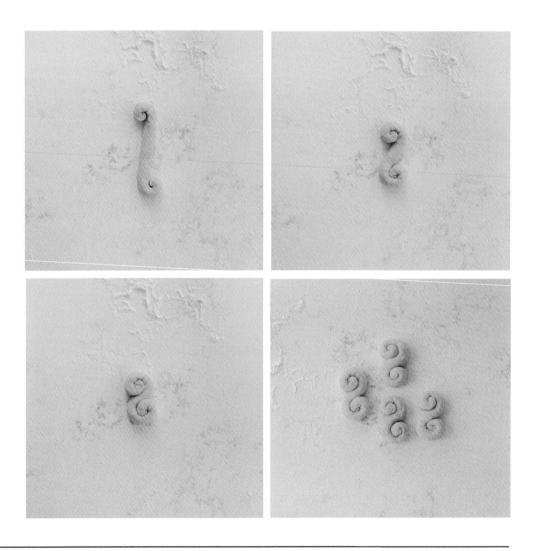

King Cake

The wreath-shaped king cake, swirled with fruits and topped with colored sugar, symbolizes the crowns of the three wise kings at the Nativity. Although king cake is most popularly associated with Mardi Gras in New Orleans, it is also served in countries such as Portugal and Spain (Roscón de Reyes) for the festival of Epiphany—at the end of the Christmas season—and up until Lent. One slice of cake traditionally contains a small figure representing the baby Jesus, and the recipient of this slice will have good luck for the rest of the year. In Louisiana, these European traditions have melded with Creole and Caribbean cultures, producing varieties of king cake that contain coconut, praline, and berries.

Makes 1 round loaf

1½ pounds (small cantaloupe-size portion) Brioche dough (page 65), Challah dough (page 147), Amish-Style Milk Bread dough (page 83), or any other enriched dough in the book
½ cup sugar
1 teaspoon freshly grated nutmeg
1 teaspoon ground cinnamon
1 cup raisins (optional)
Egg yolk wash (1 egg yolk beaten with 1 tablespoon water), for brushing the loaf
1 almond, bean, or plastic king cake baby, for a trinket

GLAZE
2 cups confectioners' sugar
2 tablespoons heavy cream
1 drop orange or almond extract

Purple, green, and gold colored sugars, sprinkles, or dragees (edible gold balls), for decorating the loaf

1. To bake: Line a baking sheet with parchment paper or a silicone mat. In a small bowl, mix together the sugar, nutmeg, and cinnamon.

2. Dust the surface of the refrigerated dough with flour and cut off a 1½-pound (small cantaloupe-size) piece. Dust the piece with more flour and quickly shape into a ball by stretching the surface of the dough around to the bottom, rotating the ball a quarter-turn as you go.

3. Using a rolling pin, roll the dough out to a ¼-inch-thick rectangle, about 11 × 15 inches. Cover the dough with the sugar mixture and scatter the raisins (if using) and trinket over the top.

4. Starting on the long side, roll the dough up into a long rope.

5. Pinch together the 2 ends, place the ring on the prepared baking sheet, cover loosely with plastic wrap, and allow to rest at room temperature for 90 minutes.

6. Preheat the oven to 350°F, with a rack placed in the center of the oven.

7. Brush the top with egg wash and bake for 35 to 40 minutes.

8. Allow the bread to cool completely.

9. Make the glaze: Mix the confectioners' sugar, heavy cream, and extract until smooth.

10. Spoon the glaze over the loaf. Sprinkle the colored sugar over the glaze before it has a chance to set.

13

EASTER BREADS

Around the world, Easter is an exuberant time of renewed hope and a celebration of the resurrection of Christ from the dead. On the Greek island of Corfu, people throw clay pots off their balconies to symbolize getting rid of the old to make room for better things to come. Christians in western India make marzipan Easter eggs to give to friends, while in the French town of Haux, villagers gather in the main square to feast on a giant omelet. Easter is a time for new beginnings and fresh starts, and of course . . . delicious meals. We find that Easter breads tend to have especially innovative and unique shapes, usually laden with the symbolism of the holiday.

Greek Easter Twist with Colored Eggs (Tsoureki)

Tsoureki is a braided bread with red-dyed eggs baked into it. The red eggs are reminders of the blood Jesus shed; this vibrant color has been a tradition in Eastern Europe for centuries. The bread gets its distinctive aroma from the Greek spices *mahlepi* and *mastic* but is also delicious with aniseed or cardamom.

Although red eggs are traditional, it is fun to dye them with other colors as well. Kids will enjoy being creative with the colors and helping with the twisted dough.

Makes I loaf

2 pounds (cantaloupe-size portion) Challah dough (page 147) or Brioche dough (page 65) dough (When you mix the dough, add 1 teaspoon mahlepi or ground aniseed and 2 teaspoons grated orange zest to the water.)

All-purpose flour, for dusting

5 dyed eggs (see page 271)

Egg wash (1 egg beaten with 1 tablespoon water), for brushing the loaf

Decorating sugar, for sprinkling on the loaf (optional)

1. Dust the surface of the refrigerated dough with flour and cut off a 1½-pound (small cantaloupe–size) piece. Dust the piece with more flour and quickly shape it into a rough ball by stretching the surface of the dough around to the bottom, rotating the ball a quarter-turn as you go. Divide the dough into 2 pieces.

2. Stretch the 2 pieces into ropes. If the dough is not stretching easily, just let it sit on the counter for about 5 minutes.

3. Continue stretching until each rope is about 1 inch thick and about 30 inches long.

Pinch the ropes together at 1 end and twist them together tightly. Join the 2 ends together to form a ring.

4. Gently transfer to a baking sheet lined with parchment paper. Stretch the twisted dough apart in 5 places and fit an egg in each space; make sure the eggs are evenly spaced around the ring. Cover loosely with plastic wrap and allow to rest at room temperature for 90 minutes.

5. Preheat the oven to 350°F, with a rack placed in the center of the oven.

6. Brush the dough with egg wash and sprinkle with sugar (if using), avoiding the eggs.

7. Bake for 35 to 40 minutes, or until the loaf is golden brown.

8. Allow the loaf to cool on a wire rack.

DYED EGGS: Combine 2 cups boiling water, 2 teaspoons vinegar, and food coloring in a bowl. Drop the hard-boiled eggs into the dye. If you are interested in using natural dyes to color your eggs, turmeric, beet juice, and indigo flowers create nice colors, but are not as bright as food dye and require being left in the solution for about 30 minutes to really take on color. The longer you leave them, the brighter they will be.

"I stir my bread dough with a Danish dough whisk. One evening, I was teaching this method and a student laughed and said, 'My wife bought me one of those and I had no idea what it was, so I use it to retrieve hard boiled eggs from the boiling water!' Well, that struck me as a brilliant idea, so when I dropped the eggs in the dye and had nothing to pluck them out with, I thought of him and grabbed my whisk. Worked like a charm" —Zoë

Make sure your eggs are well rinsed so they don't bleed color onto the bread.

VARIATION: INDIVIDUAL TSOUREKI

Makes 6 mini tsoureki

Follow the Greek Easter Twist recipe, but use 1 pound of dough and 6 dyed eggs. Divide the dough into 6 equal balls. Form the ropes, twist them, and form the rings as directed, making the ropes ½ inch thick and 10 inches long. Cover, allow to rest for 40 minutes, and then brush with egg wash, sprinkle with sugar, and place a dyed egg in the center. Bake for about 25 minutes, or until golden brown.

Fennel-Scented Easter Bread
(Folar de Pascoa)

Folar de Páscoa, popular in Portugal, is a simple, round bread with hard-boiled eggs resting on top. The eggs are secured to the bread with a dough cross that will also serve as a decoration for the finished loaf. Fennel, an herb native to the Mediterranean, is an unexpected and subtle addition to the dough, giving off a slight licorice taste.

I pound (grapefruit-size portion) Challah dough (page 147), Brioche dough (page 65), or any other enriched dough in the book

All-purpose flour, for dusting

I teaspoon ground fennel seed

4 hard-boiled eggs, in the shell

Egg wash (I egg beaten with I tablespoon water)

1. Dust the surface of the refrigerated dough with flour and cut off a 1-pound (grapefruit-size) piece. Using a rolling pin, roll the dough out to a ¼-inch-thick rectangle, about 9 × 12 inches. Spread the ground fennel over the dough. Roll the dough up into a log and then form it into a ball. Knead the ball for a few minutes to distribute the fennel throughout the dough.

2. Take off a 2-ounce piece (golf-ball size). Dust the large piece with more flour and quickly shape it into a ball by stretching the surface of the dough around to the bottom, rotating the ball a quarter-turn as you go. Divide the small dough piece in half. Form each half into an 8-inch rope. Flatten the ropes.

3. Set the large ball of dough on a baking sheet lined with parchment paper and flatten it so it is about 1 inch thick. Place the eggs on the dough so they won't touch. Lay the 2 flattened ropes over the eggs to form a cross.

Visit BreadIn5.com, where you'll find recipes, photos, videos, and instructional material.

273

4. Cover loosely with plastic wrap and allow to rest at room temperature for 60 minutes.

5. Preheat the oven to 350°F, with a rack placed in the center of the oven.

6. Brush with egg wash, avoiding the eggs.

7. Bake for 30 to 40 minutes, until golden brown and set.

8. Allow to cool on a rack before serving.

Hot Cross Buns

These crowd-pleasing buns hail from the British Isles, where they are eaten on Good Friday. Even before the introduction of Christianity to England, Saxons made buns marked with a cross to celebrate the goddess Eostre, the namesake of this holiday, a tradition which was later incorporated into the celebration of the Resurrection. Many legends surround hot cross buns. For example, some believe that hot cross buns baked for Easter will never go bad and can be kept as a good luck charm. Some chefs even claim that keeping a leftover bun hanging in the kitchen prevents breads from getting burnt. We think an oven timer works better for that, but we do know that this recipe will satisfy your Easter sweet tooth every year.

INGREDIENT	VOLUME (U.S.)	WEIGHT (U.S.)	WEIGHT (METRIC)
Lukewarm water (100°F or below)	1½ cups	12 ounces	340 grams
Granulated yeast[1]	1 tablespoon	0.35 ounce	10 grams
Kosher salt[1]	1 tablespoon	0.6 ounce	17 grams
Large eggs, lightly beaten	8	1 pound	455 grams
Honey	½ cup	6 ounces	170 grams
Unsalted butter, melted, plus butter for greasing the pan	1½ cups (3 sticks)	12 ounces	340 grams
All-purpose flour	7½ cups	2 pounds, 5½ ounces	1,065 grams
Ground cinnamon	2 teaspoons		
Freshly grated nutmeg	1 teaspoon		
Ground allspice	1 teaspoon		
Orange zest, grated	2 teaspoons		
Pure vanilla extract	2 teaspoons		
Currants or raisins	1½ cups	7 ounces	200 grams
Egg wash (1 egg yolk with 1 tablespoon water), for brushing buns			

[1]Can decrease (see pages 15 and 33).

ICING

4 ounces cream cheese

2 ounces unsalted butter, room temperature

½ cup confectioners' sugar

¼ cup maple syrup

1. Mixing and storing the dough: Mix the water, yeast, salt, eggs, honey, and melted butter in a 6-quart bowl, or a lidded (not airtight) food container.

2. Mix in the flour, spices, zest, vanilla extract, and raisins without kneading, using a spoon or a heavy-duty stand mixer (with paddle). If you're not using a machine, you may need to use wet hands to incorporate the last bit of flour. The dough will be loose but will firm up when chilled; don't try to work with it before chilling.

3. Cover (not airtight), and allow to rest at room temperature for 2 hours, then refrigerate.

4. The dough can be used as soon as it's thoroughly chilled, at least 3 hours. Refrigerate the container and use over the next 5 days. To freeze dough, see page 42.

5. On baking day, dust the surface of the refrigerated dough with flour and cut off a 2-pound (cantaloupe-size) piece. Divide the dough into 9 equal pieces and quickly shape into balls.

6. Place 2 inches apart on a baking sheet lined with parchment paper or a silicone mat, cover loosely with plastic wrap and allow to rest at room temperature for about 45 minutes.

7. Preheat the over to 350°F, with a rack placed in the center of the oven.

8. Brush the tops with egg wash and place the baking sheet in the oven. Bake for about 25 minutes, or until richly browned.

9. To make the icing, mix the cream cheese, butter, confectioners' sugar, and maple syrup in a small bowl.

10. Allow to cool completely. Pipe the icing in a cross over the top of each bun. There will be extra icing for spreading on the buns.

Kulich

Kulich, an Easter bread enjoyed around Eastern Europe and Russia, can be recognized by its tall base and rounded top, as well as a generous coating of sugar glaze. Some say that the overflowing muffin top of this bread represents the dome of a church. In the Russian Orthodox tradition, kulich is surrounded by flowers and receives a special blessing at midnight mass before Easter Sunday. This dough is lightly flavored with saffron, an exotic spice that traditionally would have only been used on special occasions.

To get the traditional shape, the bread needs to be baked in a cylindrical mold, a coffee can, or a paper panettone mold (see page 27).

Makes 1 loaf

2 pounds (cantaloupe-size portion) Saint Lucia Saffron Buns dough (page 261)

All-purpose flour, for dusting

Egg wash (1 egg beaten with 1 tablespoon water), for brushing the dough

ICING

½ cup confectioners' sugar

2 tablespoons cream (or more as needed for a thick but pourable consistency)

Colorful sprinkles, for top (to represent the colorful flowers)

1. To bake: Generously grease a panettone mold with butter. Dust the surface of the refrigerated dough with flour and cut off a 2-pound (cantaloupe-size) piece. Dust the piece with more flour and quickly shape it into a ball by stretching the surface of the dough around to the bottom, rotating the ball a quarter-turn as you go. Place the ball in a greased panettone mold, seam side down.

2. Cover loosely with plastic wrap and allow to rest at room temperature for 90 minutes.

3. Preheat the oven to 350°F, with a rack placed in the center of the oven.

4. Brush the dough with egg wash. Bake for 50 to 55 minutes, or until golden brown.

5. Allow to cool on a rack.

6. Make the icing: Mix the confectioners' sugar and heavy cream together until smooth and thick enough to cling to the cake. You don't want it to drip off the sides. Drizzle the icing over the cake and cover with colorful sprinkles.

Romanian Easter Braid with Ricotta Custard (Pasca)

This Romanian Easter bread is the perfect marriage of two of our favorite foods. A brioche braid encases a rich ricotta cheesecake. It sounds difficult to make, but as long as you can braid the dough, you can master this beauty. The sweet cheese filling is traditionally made with raisins and rum, but if you'd rather leave them out or swap them with chocolate chips, we're all for that.

Makes 1 cake

1 pound (grapefruit-size portion) Brioche dough (page 65), Challah dough (page 147),
    Amish-Style Milk Bread dough (page 83), or any other enriched dough in the book
All-purpose flour, for dusting
Egg yolk wash (1 yolk beaten with 1 tablespoon water), for brushing the loaf

FILLING
¾ cup whole-milk ricotta
⅓ cup sugar
2 large eggs
1 teaspoon grated orange zest
½ teaspoon grated lemon zest
2 tablespoons rum or milk (if you don't use rum, add 1 teaspoon pure vanilla extract)
¾ cup raisins
1 tablespoon honey mixed with 1 teaspoon cream, for glazing the loaf

1. To bake: Grease a 9-inch springform cake pan. Dust the surface of the refrigerated dough with flour and cut off a 1-pound (grapefruit-size) piece. Dust the piece with more flour and quickly shape it into a ball by stretching the surface of the dough around to the bottom, rotating the ball a quarter-turn as you go. Divide the dough into 4 equal pieces and form them into balls.

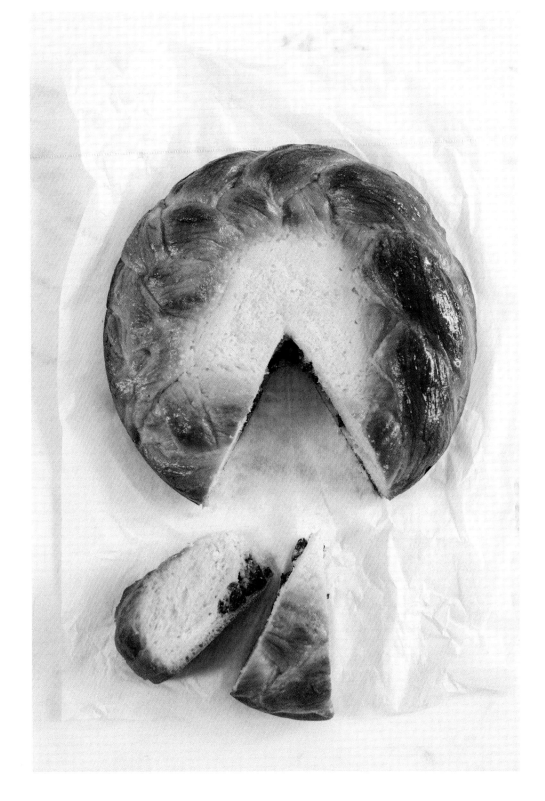

2. Roll one of the balls of dough into a disk that fits the bottom of the springform pan. It will be very thin.

3. Gently roll and stretch each of the remaining dough balls, dusting with flour so your hands don't stick to it, until you have 3 ropes about ½ inch thick and 20 inches long. You may need to let the dough relax for about 5 minutes so it won't resist your efforts.

4. Braiding the dough: Lay the ropes side by side, pinch them together at one end, and then pull the left strand over the center strand and lay it down.

5. Now pull the right strand over the center strand. Continue, alternating outer strands and always pulling the outer strands into the middle, never moving what becomes the center strand. When you get to the end, pinch the strands together (see page 149).

6. Stretch the braid gently so that it will fit in the pan as a circle, with the ends overlapping so they are the same height as the rest of the circle of dough. Cover loosely with plastic wrap and allow to rest at room temperature for 45 minutes.

7. Preheat the oven to 350°F, with a rack placed in the center of the oven.

8. Prepare the filling: In a large bowl, whisk together the ricotta, sugar, eggs, orange and lemon zests, and rum. Stir in the raisins. Stretch the braid to fit against the pan. Pour the filling in the center of the risen dough. Don't allow it to go over the top of the dough.

9. Brush the dough with egg yolk wash.

10. Bake for about 30 minutes. The pasca is done when it is a deep caramel color and the filling is set.

11. Allow to cool slightly on a rack before removing from the pan. Brush with honey glaze.

12. Serve warm or at room temperature.

Easter Raisin Bread (Mazanec)

Sweetened with rum-soaked raisins and topped with almonds, this bread evokes colorful Easter traditions of the Czech Republic. Rural villages produce intricate Easter eggs (*kraslice*), and shops all over the country sell pussy willow branches, symbolic of fertility and youth. Families usually eat *mazanec* with jam and butter for breakfast on Easter morning, but these golden-crusted rounds will help any morning feel a little more special.

Makes at least three 1½-pound loaves

INGREDIENT	VOLUME (U.S.)	WEIGHT (U.S.)	WEIGHT (METRIC)
Brandy	⅓ cup	3 ounces	85 grams
Raisins	1½ cups	7 ounces	200 grams
Lukewarm whole milk (100°F or below)	1¼ cups	10 ounces	285 grams
Granulated yeast[1]	1 tablespoon	0.35 ounce	10 grams
Kosher salt[1]	1 tablespoon	0.6 ounce	17 grams
Sugar	¾ cup	6 ounces	170 grams
Large eggs, lightly beaten	6	12 ounces	340 grams
Unsalted butter, melted and slightly cooled	1 cup (2 sticks)	8 ounces	225 grams
Lemon extract	1 teaspoon		
Pure vanilla extract	2 teaspoons		
Lemon zest, grated	2 teaspoons		
Almond paste, cut into ¼-inch cubes	1 cup	8 ounces	230 grams
All-purpose flour	6½ cups	2 pounds	910 grams

(Continued)			
Ground mace	½ teaspoon		
Egg glaze (1 egg yolk beaten with 1 tablespoon milk), for brushing the loaf			
Sliced almonds, for sprinkling on the loaf	¼ cup		
Sugar, for sprinkling on the loaf			

¹Can decrease (see pages 15 and 33).

1. Mixing and storing the dough: In a small bowl, combine the brandy and raisins. Heat in the microwave for 1 minute and let sit for about 30 minutes.

2. Mix the yeast, salt, sugar, eggs, melted butter, extracts, and lemon zest with the water in a 6-quart bowl or a lidded (not airtight) food container. Mix in the brandy soaked raisins, with any remaining liquid, and the almond paste.

3. Mix in the flour and mace without kneading, using a heavy-duty stand mixer (with paddle), a Danish dough whisk, or a spoon. If you're not using a machine, you may need to use wet hands to incorporate the last bit of flour. The dough will be loose but will firm up when chilled (don't try to use it without chilling).

4. Cover (not airtight), allow to rest at room temperature for 2 hours, and then refrigerate.

5. The dough can be used as soon as it's thoroughly chilled after the initial rise or frozen for later use. Refrigerate the container and use over the next 5 days. To freeze dough, see page 42.

6. On baking day, line a baking sheet with parchment paper or a silicone mat.

7. Dust the surface of the refrigerated dough with flour and cut off a 1½-pound (small cantaloupe–size) piece. Dust the piece with more flour and quickly shape it into a ball by stretching the surface of the dough around to the bottom, rotating the ball a quarter-turn as you go. Place the ball on the baking sheet, seam side down.

8. Cover loosely with plastic wrap and allow to rest at room temperature for 90 minutes.

9. Preheat the oven to 350°F, with a rack placed in the center of the oven.

10. Brush the loaf with egg glaze and sprinkle sliced almonds and sugar over the loaf. Slash a ½-inch deep cross on the top of the loaf. Bake for about 45 minutes, or until golden brown and hollow-sounding when tapped.

11. Allow to cool on a rack before slicing and eating.

Paska

Paska is eaten in many Eastern European Christian countries, especially Ukraine. A tall, cylindrical bread, it stands out for its decorated top. Traditionally, the top has intricate braiding, which represents the Trinity, but we went with a more ornate swirl of dough. Since paska is only eaten once a year, it is traditionally baked in a meditative and prayerful silence, and the bakers try to rid their minds of unkind thoughts while they work. Like *kulich,* paska is bundled up and brought to mass before Easter to be blessed by a priest. At a typical Ukrainian table, paska might be surrounded by a centerpiece of *pysanka,* or dyed eggs.

Paska can be baked as individual buns or as a large loaf; we include both sizes. No matter which size you go with, you'll want to fill the pan three-quarters full.

Makes 8 buns

2 pounds (cantaloupe-size) Brioche dough (page 65), Challah dough (page 147), Amish-
   Style Milk Bread dough (page 83), or any other enriched dough in the book
All-purpose flour, for dusting
Egg wash (I egg beaten with I tablespoon water), for brushing the buns

1. To bake: Butter 8 muffin tins. Dust the surface of the refrigerated dough with flour and cut off a 2-pound (cantaloupe-size) piece. Divide the dough into 9 equal pieces. Dust 8 of the pieces with more flour and quickly shape each of them into a ball by stretching the surface of the dough around to the bottom, rotating the ball a quarter-turn as you go. Place the balls in a buttered mold, seam side down.

2. Cover loosely with plastic wrap and allow to rest at room temperature for 60 minutes Also cover the remaining piece of dough.

3. Preheat the oven to 350°F, with a rack placed in the center of the oven.

4. Brush the dough with egg wash.

5. Using a rolling pin, roll the remaining small piece of dough out to a ⅛-inch-thick rectangle, about 4 × 12 inches, and cut into strips. Roll up each strip to form a coil and

place them on the top of each small loaf in a decorative pattern. Brush the coils with egg wash.

6. Bake in the center of the oven for 30 minutes, or until golden brown and hollow-sounding when tapped. The amount of dough and baking times will vary depending on the mold size.

7. Allow to cool on a rack before slicing and eating.

VARIATION: LARGE PASKA

To make one large loaf, use 1½ pounds dough and pull off a 4-ounce piece for decorating the top. Shape the dough as directed in the Paska recipe, place it in a panettone mold, and proceed with the remaining directions. Cover, allow to rest for 75 minutes, and bake for 45 to 50 minutes.

14

CELEBRATION AND BRUNCH BREADS

Raspberry Star Bread

When Sarah Kieffer baked a version of this for our website, it blew our minds how gorgeous it was, and we just knew a star bread had to be in a book about celebrations. It is an obvious choice for Christmas morning, since it looks just like an ornament, but we didn't put it with the Christmas breads because we think it should be made all year long. This one is filled with Quick Raspberry Jam, and we've also included the one Sarah created with cinnamon and sugar as a variation.

Makes 1 large loaf

2 pounds (cantaloupe-size portion) Brioche dough (page 65),
    Amish-Style Milk Bread dough (page 83), or Challah dough (page 147),
    or any other enriched dough in the book
All-purpose flour, for dusting
1 cup Quick Raspberry Jam (page 351)

Egg wash (1 egg beaten with 1 tablespoon water), for brushing the dough
Decorating sugar, for sprinkling on the loaf

1. Dust the surface of the refrigerated dough with flour and cut off a 2-pound (canta-loupe-size) piece. Divide the piece in 4 equal pieces, dust with more flour and quickly shape them into balls by stretching the surface of the dough around to the bottom, rotating the ball a quarter-turn as you go.

2. Roll the dough balls out into 4 rounds about 10 inches wide. As you roll out the dough, add flour as needed to prevent sticking.

3. Place one of the dough rounds on a piece of parchment paper. Top with one-third of the raspberry jam. Repeat with next 2 layers of dough and raspberry jam. Top with the final layer of dough.

4. Place a 2½-inch biscuit cutter (or anything that size and round) in the center of the dough. Use a knife or bench scraper to divide the circle in 16 equal sections, leaving the biscuit cutter in place so you don't cut all the way to the center.

5. Twist 2 of the sections away from each other with 2 rotations, then pinch the 2 sections together at the end to form a point. Continue with the rest of the sections until you have 8 points.

6. Cover loosely with plastic wrap and allow to rest at room temperature for 90 minutes.

7. Preheat the oven to 375°F, with a rack placed in the center of the oven.

8. Transfer the parchment paper with the star onto a baking sheet. Brush the exposed dough with egg wash and sprinkle decorating sugar in the center of the loaf.

9. Bake for 25 to 30 minutes until golden brown and set.

10. Allow to cool on a rack before serving.

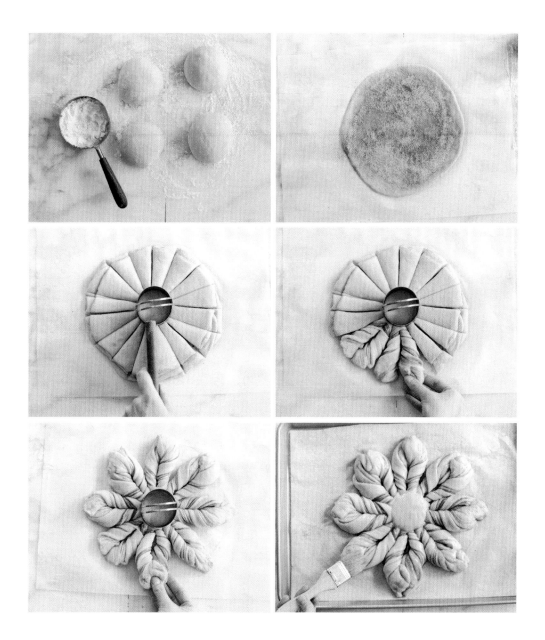

VARIATION: **CINNAMON STAR BREAD**

Mix ½ cup sugar with 1 tablespoon ground cinnamon. Follow the Raspberry Star Bread recipe, but replace the raspberry jam with the cinnamon sugar, spreading one-third of the sugar mixture on each of the first 3 layers.

Dutch Crunch

Dutch Crunch gets its name from a similar bread found in the Netherlands, which is called tiger bread (*tijgerbrood* or *tijgerbol*). It's easy to see how it got that name. The spots are created by covering the dough with a slurry of rice flour, sugar, yeast, and toasted sesame oil. The fragrance of the sesame oil is fantastic, and the slightly sweet crispy bits on the loaf are hard to resist snacking on before you even cut into the bread.

Makes I loaf

I pound (grapefruit-size portion) Amish-Style Milk Bread dough (page 83), White Bread Master Recipe dough (page 48), Challah dough (page 147) or Brioche dough (page 65) dough

All-purpose flour, for dusting

TOPPING

½ cup warm water

I tablespoon yeast

⅔ cup rice flour

2 tablespoons sugar

¼ teaspoon salt

I tablespoon vegetable oil

I teaspoon toasted sesame oil

1. Dust the surface of the refrigerated dough with flour and cut off a 1-pound (grapefruit-size) piece. Dust the piece with more flour and quickly shape it into a ball by stretching the surface of the dough around to the bottom, rotating the ball a quarter-turn as you go.

2. Place the dough on a piece of parchment paper and allow to rest for 75 minutes.

3. Preheat the oven to 350°F, with a rack placed in the center of the oven.

4. Make the topping: As the dough is resting, mix all the topping ingredients in a large bowl and cover with plastic. The yeast will make the topping double in volume, so make sure it has enough room to grow.

5. Once the topping has doubled in size (which conveniently takes about the same amount of time as it takes for the dough to rise), spread about ½ cup of the mixture evenly over the dough; the topping will collapse when you spread it. You can store the remaining topping for a week in the refrigerator, well covered (but vented to prevent pressure buildup).

6. Bake for about 35 minutes, or until the crust is golden brown.

7. Allow to cool on a rack before serving

Pan de Muerto

Día de Muertos is a Mexican holiday dedicated to honoring deceased loved ones. Versions of this holiday have been observed since Aztec times. During the three days of Día de Muertos, Mexican families use marigolds, skull-shaped confections, and incense to decorate altars at their relatives' graves. The altars are meant to entice the spirits of the dead to return for a visit to earth and hear the prayers of their living family members. *Pan de Muerto* is a soft, sweet bun eaten during Día de Muertos or left at altars. This custom reflects an acceptance of the cycle of life and death and the joy that can be found in remembering those who have passed away.

Makes I loaf

  1 pound (grapefruit-size portion) Challah dough (page 147) or any other enriched dough
    in the book
All-purpose flour, for dusting
Egg wash (1 egg beaten with 1 tablespoon water), for brushing the dough
2 tablespoons apricot jam
¼ cup sugar
1 drop orange blossom water or orange oil

1. To bake: Line a baking sheet with parchment paper or a silicone mat.

2. Dust the surface of the refrigerated dough with flour and cut off a 1-pound (grapefruit-size) piece. Dust the piece with more flour and quickly shape it into a ball by stretching the surface of the dough around to the bottom, rotating the ball a quarter-turn as you go. Pinch off a 3-ounce piece from the bottom. Place the larger ball on the baking sheet, seam side down, cover loosely with plastic wrap, and allow to rest at room temperature for 90 minutes.

3. Divide the smaller ball in half. Form one half into a ball. Divide the remaining dough into 5 equal pieces and elongate them into 2-inch ropes. Place the ball and ropes on a floured surface, cover loosely with plastic wrap, and allow to rest at room temperature for 30 minutes.

4. Once they have rested, press 2 fingers into each rope, indenting the dough in thirds. Roll the dough back and forth until the dough is quite thin in those spots. Repeat with the remaining ropes.

5. Preheat the oven to 350°F, with a rack placed in the center of the oven.

6. Brush the large ball of dough with egg wash and place the indented ropes over the loaf, equally spaced, radiating out from the center like the spokes of a wheel. Brush the ropes with egg wash and place the small ball at the top, where the ropes come together. Brush the whole loaf with egg wash again. Bake in the center of the oven for about 35 minutes, or until golden brown and hollow-sounding when tapped.

7. When the loaf comes from the oven, heat the apricot jam and brush it over the loaf. Combine the sugar and orange blossom water by rubbing them together between your fingers. Sprinkle the scented sugar over the loaf. Allow to cool on a rack before slicing and eating.

Apple-Cranberry Coffee Cake

This cake is best made with sweet apples (page 359) to contrast the tanginess of the cranberries. It is the perfect balance of flavors: the soft baked fruit is contrasted nicely with the crunch of the oat streusel. Serve with a scoop of ice cream, a dollop of whipped cream, or just on its own, and it's a perfect cake for a fall gathering.

Makes 1 coffee cake

OAT STREUSEL TOPPING

½ cup oats

½ cup all-purpose flour

½ cup well-packed brown sugar

½ cup chopped nuts (optional)

4 tablespoons (½ stick) melted unsalted butter

Pinch salt

½ teaspoon ground cinnamon

CAKE

3 small apples, quartered and thinly sliced (see page 361 for apples)

1½ cups fresh cranberries

¼ cup well-packed brown sugar

Grated zest of ½ orange

1 pound (grapefruit-size portion) Brioche dough (page 65), Amish-Style Milk Bread dough (page 83), Challah dough (page 147), or any other enriched dough in the book

All-purpose flour, for dusting

1. Prepare the oat streusel topping: Combine all the streusel ingredients in a bowl and mix until the butter is roughly incorporated. Don't overmix—you want a crumbly texture. Set aside.

2. Assemble the cake: Grease an 8-inch springform cake pan with butter and dust with flour. Set aside.

3. Toss the apples, cranberries, brown sugar, and orange zest together in a small bowl, and set aside.

4. Dust the surface of the refrigerated dough with flour and cut off a 1-pound (grapefruit-size) piece. Divide the piece in two, dust with more flour, and quickly shape each piece into a rough ball by stretching the surface of the dough around to the bottom, rotating the ball a quarter-turn as you go.

5. Roll the dough balls out into two ¼-inch-thick rounds, about 9 inches across. As you roll out the dough, add flour as needed to prevent sticking.

6. Place one of the dough rounds in the bottom of the prepared cake pan. Top with half the apple-cranberry mixture and then sprinkle half the streusel topping over it. Repeat with the remaining dough round, apple-cranberry mixture, and streusel.

7. Cover loosely with plastic wrap and allow to rest at room temperature for 90 minutes.

9. Preheat the oven to 350°F, with a rack placed in the center of the oven.

10. Bake for 55 to 60 minutes.

11. Allow to cool for 15 minutes. While the cake is still warm, remove from the springform pan.

12. Serve warm or at room temperature.

Blueberry Coffee Cake

This cake is made with layers of rich dough, crunchy streusel, and tart but sweet home-made blueberry quick jam. The beauty of a quick jam is that it isn't too firm and it's not overly sweet. If you want to make this cake with store-bought jam, we recommend folding in some fresh blueberries to reduce the sweetness.

Makes 1 coffee cake

CAKE

Butter, for greasing the pan

All-purpose flour, for dusting

1 pound (grapefruit-size portion) Brioche dough (page 65), Whole Wheat Brioche dough (page 68), or any other enriched dough in the book

1 cup Quick Blueberry Jam (page 353), or ¾ cup store-bought blueberry jam plus ½ cup fresh or frozen blueberries

Streusel topping (below)

STREUSEL TOPPING

⅓ cup all-purpose flour

⅓ cup well-packed brown sugar

¼ teaspoons ground cinnamon

Pinch salt

2 tablespoons unsalted butter, softened

1. Assemble the cake: Grease an 8-inch springform cake pan with butter and dust with flour. Set aside.

2. Dust the surface of the refrigerated dough with flour and cut off a 1-pound (grape-fruit-size) piece. Divide the piece into 3 pieces, dust with more flour and quickly shape them into balls by stretching the surface of the dough around to the bottom, rotating the ball a quarter-turn as you go.

3. Roll the dough balls out into 3 rounds to fit the pan. As you roll out the dough, add flour as needed to prevent sticking.

4. Place one of the dough rounds in the bottom of the prepared cake pan. Top with one-third of the blueberry jam. Repeat with next 2 layers of dough and the remaining blueberry jam.

5. Cover loosely with plastic wrap and allow to rest at room temperature for 90 minutes.

6. Make the streusel topping: While the coffee cake is resting, mix together the flour, brown sugar, cinnamon, and salt. Add the soft butter and work it into the sugar mixture with your fingers. Squeeze the streusel to form some small clumps, which gives the topping some nice texture when it bakes. Sprinkle it over the top of the cake.

7. Preheat the oven to 350°F, with a rack placed in the center of the oven.

8. Bake for about 50 minutes, or until the streusel is golden and the cake is set in the center.

9. Allow to cool for 10 to 15 minutes. While the cake is still warm, remove from the springform pan.

10. Serve warm or at room temperature.

Kolache

When Czech immigrants came to the United States in the nineteenth and early twentieth centuries, they brought the *kolache,* a buttery roll filled with fruit or poppy seeds. Once the dessert of simple peasants, kolache came to be served at occasions ranging from church fundraisers to weddings. Even today, Czech-American communities across the Great Plains, including New Prague in our own home state of Minnesota, celebrate their heritage with annual kolache festivals. The world's largest known kolache, weighing in at 2,605 pounds, was made in Prague, Nebraska, but your family will be just as impressed by these bite-sized versions.

Makes eight 3-inch pastries

1½ pounds (small cantaloupe–size portion) Amish-Style Milk Bread dough (page 83), Challah dough (page 147), or any other enriched dough in the book

All-purpose flour, for dusting

Egg wash (1 egg beaten with 1 tablespoon water), for brushing the loaf

1 cup filling (pick fillings from chapter 17, such as Almond Cream page 357, Applesauce page 358, or Prune Filling page 360, and there are more to choose from)

1. Line a baking sheet with parchment paper or a silicone mat.

2. Dust the surface of the refrigerated dough with flour and cut off a 1½-pound (small cantaloupe–size) piece. Dust the piece with more flour and quickly shape it into a rough ball by stretching the surface of the dough around to the bottom, rotating the ball a quarter-turn as you go.

3. Using a rolling pin, roll the dough out to a ½-inch-thick rectangle, about 8 × 9 inches, adding flour as needed to prevent sticking.

4. Using a 3-inch round cookie cutter, cut out about a dozen circles. (Save the scraps to use in Cinnamon Twists and Turns, page 196, or return them to the bucket of dough to use later.)

5. Lay the dough rounds on the prepared baking sheet, cover loosely with plastic wrap, and allow to rest at room temperature for 45 minutes; they should be very soft and puffy.

6. Preheat the oven to 350°F, with a rack placed in the center of the oven.

7. Make an indent in the middle of each dough round, about 1½ inches in diameter. Fill that indent with 2 tablespoons of your prepared filling of choice. Brush the exposed edges with the egg wash.

8. Bake the pastries for about 20 minutes, or until the dough is golden brown.

9. Serve warm or cooled.

Visit BreadIn5.com, where you'll find recipes, photos, videos, and instructional material.

311

Raspberry Braid

This braid is a showstopper and looks like you spent all day preparing it. The truth is, it's really easy and fast to make and is the perfect sweet to bring to a brunch or book club. The brightness of the raspberries combined with the creamy layer of cream cheese is a wonderful pairing, but you should play with the flavor combinations; another favorite is pastry cream (page 354) with a cherry Quick Jam (page 353). You'll also want to try the almond cream and apricot variation (below). Turn to the Quick Jams and Fillings chapter (page 351) for even more inspiration. You can also make it using our flaky Danish-ish Dough (page 334).

Makes 1 loaf

1 pound (grapefruit-size portion) Amish-Style Milk Bread dough (page 83), Challah dough
   (page 147), Danish-ish Dough (page 334), or any other enriched dough in the book
All-purpose flour, for dusting

CREAM CHEESE FILLING
4 ounces cream cheese
½ teaspoon grated lemon zest
1 tablespoon sugar
¾ cup Quick Raspberry Jam (page 351), or your favorite store-bought jam
Egg yolk wash (1 egg yolk beaten with 1 tablespoon water), for brushing the braid

RASPBERRY ICING
½ cup confectioners' sugar
2 tablespoons heavy cream (or more as needed to reach the proper consistency)
6 ounces raspberries, for garnish and icing

1. Make the cream cheese filling: Mix the cream cheese, lemon zest, and sugar in a bowl until smooth. Set aside.

2. Line a baking sheet with parchment paper or a silicone mat.

3. Dust the surface of the refrigerated dough with flour and cut off a 1-pound (grapefruit–size) piece. Dust the piece with more flour and quickly shape it into a rough ball by stretching the surface of the dough around to the bottom, rotating the ball a quarter-turn as you go.

4. Using a rolling pin, roll the dough out to a ¼-inch-thick rectangle, about 9 × 12 inches. As you roll out the dough, add flour as needed to prevent sticking.

5. Lift the dough onto the lined baking sheet. Place the cream cheese filling down the length of the dough in a 1-inch strip in the center, and add the raspberry jam on top.

6. Using a pizza cutter, cut about ½-inch-wide strips down each side. Twist and then fold the strips, left over right, crisscrossing over the filling (see photo, page 314). Lightly press the strips together as you move down the pastry, creating a braid. Cover loosely with plastic wrap and allow to rest at room temperature for 60 minutes.

7. Preheat the oven to 350°F, with a rack placed in the center of the oven.

8. Brush the braid lightly with egg wash.

9. Bake the braid for 35 to 45 minutes, or until golden brown. Allow to cool.

10. Make the raspberry glaze: While the braid is cooling, mix together the confectioners' sugar, cream, and raspberries. Add enough cream so you can drizzle the glaze from a spoon.

11. Drizzle the braid with half the glaze, cover in raspberries, and drizzle with the remaining glaze.

VARIATION: ALMOND CREAM AND APRICOT BRAID WITH ALMOND CRUNCH

½ cup raw slivered almonds

½ cup sugar

Pinch salt

½ teaspoon grated orange zest

1 teaspoon egg white

½ cup Almond Cream (page 357)

¾ cup Apricot Filling (page 360)

Mix the almonds, sugar, salt, orange zest, and egg white in a bowl. Set aside. Follow the Raspberry Braid recipe, but replace the cream cheese filling and raspberry jam with the almond cream and apricot filling. Spread the almond mixture onto the braid, and then allow to rest. Omit the egg wash; bake and cool as directed. Omit the raspberry glaze.

VARIATION: GREEK-STYLE SPINACH PIE WITH FETA AND PINE NUTS

This variation also works well with non-enriched doughs, such as the Olive Oil Dough (page 119), which can be baked at 450°F for 20 to 25 minutes. Use an egg white wash, since it doesn't burn at high temperatures.

1 pound fresh spinach, chopped

1 tablespoon olive oil

½ pound feta cheese, crumbled

⅓ cup pine nuts

Black or white sesame seeds, for
  sprinkling

1. Sauté the spinach and olive oil in a skillet over medium heat until it's wilted and has given up a good amount of liquid; drain the spinach in a sieve (to prevent a soggy bottom crust).

2. Follow the Raspberry Braid recipe, but replace the cream cheese filling and raspberry jam with the crumbled feta and drained spinach and sprinkle the pine nuts over the spinach.

3. Rest as directed. Brush with egg wash and sprinkle with sesame seeds (white seeds are fine, but the black ones are traditional in Greece and Turkey). Bake and cool as directed. Omit the raspberry glaze.

Apple Tarte Tatin

This heavenly dessert is essentially an upside-down tart. The apples caramelize in sugar and butter to produce a golden and aromatic topping. When you flip the tart, the apple juices seep down to infuse the entire dessert with sweetness. Tarte Tatin takes its name from the Tatin sisters, Stephanie and Caroline, who ran a hotel in France in the nineteenth century. According to legend, Stephanie was in the kitchen one day when she accidentally left a pan of apples on the stove too long. Trying to stop them from burning, she covered them up with pastry and put the whole thing in the oven. To her surprise, her guests demanded more—and yours will too!

Use an apple that will keep its shape and not turn to sauce as it cooks. See page 359.

Makes I tarte Tatin

3 tablespoons unsalted butter or oil (see page 12 for options)

⅓ cup (3 ounces/85 grams) well-packed brown sugar

¼ cup (3 ounces/85 grams) honey

I teaspoon fresh lemon juice

I cinnamon stick

Two I-inch round slices fresh ginger

2 whole cardamom pods (optional)

I star anise pod (optional)

8 large apples, peeled, stemmed, cored, and quartered

½ pound (orange-size portion) Brioche dough (page 65), or any other enriched dough in the book

All-purpose flour, for dusting

1. Melt the butter in a 10-inch cast-iron skillet over medium heat, and then sprinkle the sugar, honey, and lemon juice over it. Drop the cinnamon stick, ginger, cardamom

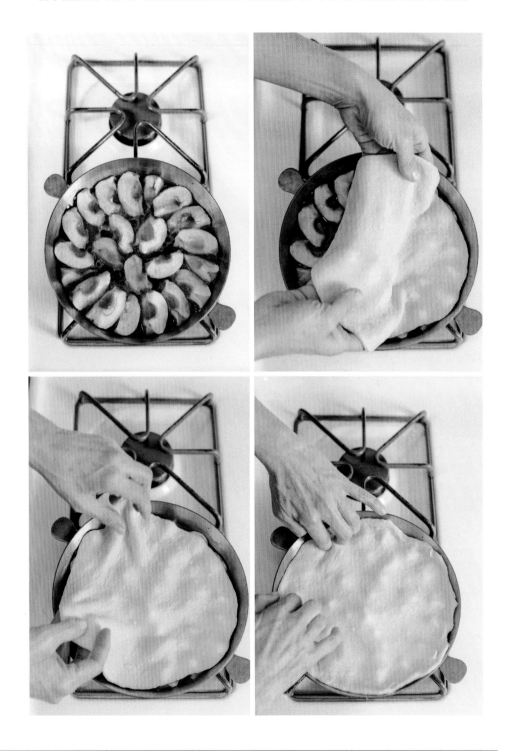

pods (if using), and star anise (if using) in the middle. Arrange the apples in a circular pattern, cut-side up, in the sugar.

2. Reduce the heat to low and cook slowly until the apples start to absorb the caramel and the juices are bubbling around them, about 30 minutes, depending on the size and firmness of the apples. Spoon the sugar over the apples as they cook. Move the apples around slightly so that they are cooked evenly. If you are using a softer apple, it will go much faster.

3. Once the apples are coloring nicely and the caramel is bubbling, turn off the heat and let them cool while you prepare the dough.

4. Preheat the oven to 350°F, with a rack placed in the center of the oven.

5. While the apples are cooling, dust the surface of the refrigerated dough with flour and cut off a ½-pound (orange-size) piece. Dust with more flour and quickly shape it into a ball by stretching the surface of the dough around to the bottom.

6. Using a rolling pin, roll the dough out into a ⅛-inch-thick round that fits the pan and extends about 1 inch beyond to allow for any shrinkage while baking. As you roll out the dough, use enough flour to prevent the dough from sticking to the work surface but not so much as to make it dry.

7. Drape the round of dough over the apples, and tuck the excess between the apples and the edge of the pan.

8. Bake for 20 to 25 minutes, or until the dough is golden brown. Remove the pan from the oven and allow the tart to cool in the skillet for about 5 minutes. Then, carefully invert it onto a serving platter that is large enough that the hot caramel juices don't spill out. Serve warm or cool.

Georgian Cheesy-Egg Boat (Khachapuri)

In the former Soviet Republic of Georgia (now an independent country nestled against the Black Sea), there's a wonderful egg, bread, and butter dish that sticks to your ribs in that cold mountainous place, and it's beautiful to look at as well. The country has many versions of enriched bread that go by this name, but this beautiful open boat–shaped one comes from the coastal southeastern Adjara region. Traditional recipes call for the sour/salty *sulguni* cheese, but we used feta cheese as a handy substitute. (Please come to the website and let us know if you find the authentic stuff.)

Makes 1 small loaf (boat)

1 tablespoon butter or oil, plus additional butter to finish, if desired

1 garlic clove, minced

4 cups (6 ounces) loosely packed fresh spinach leaves, washed and stemmed

2 tablespoons finely chopped fresh flat-leaf parsley

2 large eggs

4 ounces crumbled feta cheese

6 ounces (small orange–size portion) Super Strong Dough (page 59), Amish-Style Milk Bread dough (page 83), Light Whole Wheat Bread dough (page 77), or any other enriched dough in the book

All-purpose flour, for dusting

Salt and freshly ground black pepper

1. Preheat the oven to 400°F, with a rack placed in the center of the oven.

2. Melt the butter in a skillet; add the garlic, spinach, and parsley; and sauté until most of the water has evaporated. Allow to cool slightly. Mix one of the eggs with the cheese in a bowl.

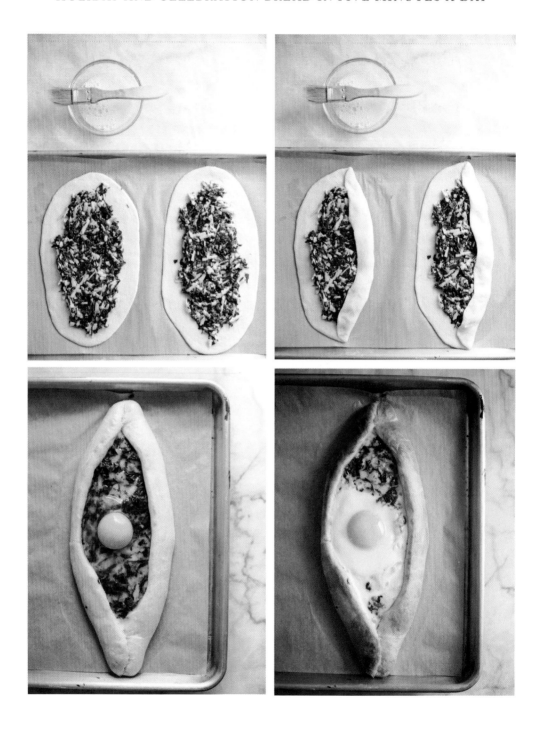

3. Dust the surface of the refrigerated dough with flour and cut off a 6-ounce (small orange–size) piece. Dust with more flour and quickly shape it into a ball by stretching the surface of the dough around to the bottom, rotating the ball a quarter-turn as you go.

4. Using your hands and a rolling pin, roll the dough out into a ⅛-inch-thick oval, about 12 inches long and 5 inches wide. Dust with flour to keep the dough from adhering to the surface. Use a dough scraper to unstick the dough as needed, and transfer to a rimmed baking sheet lined with parchment paper or a silicone mat (this will prevent egg from running everywhere if some slides off).

5. Place the filling in a line down the middle of the dough. Starting with the long side, fold the dough up over the filling; the dough will come halfway into the middle. Fold the other side over to form a boat shape. Pinch the overlapping ends together to make a good seal.

6. Brush the dough with butter and bake for 15 minutes.

7. Remove the boat from the oven. Using a large spoon, make an indentation in the cheese mixture to keep the egg from running off, and crack the remaining egg into the space.

8. Place the baking sheet back in the oven and bake, checking for doneness in 12 to 15 minutes, or until the egg is cooked to your liking. Rotate the baking sheet if one side is browning faster than the other.

9. Remove from the oven, allow to cool slightly, and brush the dough with more butter. The tradition in Adjara is to place a large pat of butter on the egg (your call). Season with salt and pepper to taste.

15

FANCY STALE BREAD

We hope you'll be baking weekly, if not daily, for all of your bread needs through the holidays and just for school lunches. If you do, you may find yourself with leftovers—here are some wonderfully tasty ways to use up that bread. They're so good, you may even find yourself baking a loaf just to create these recipes.

Bread and Butter Pudding

Bread pudding is the ultimate comfort food. It is also the perfect use for the day-old bread you will have left over when making all the recipes in this book. We like to use slightly stale bread because it absorbs the custard so well. This is excellent served à la mode or with whipped cream.

Makes 8 servings

8 egg yolks

1 cup sugar

1 quart half-and-half

¼ cup rum or brandy (optional)

1 teaspoon pure vanilla extract

¼ teaspoon freshly grated nutmeg

¼ teaspoon ground cinnamon

½ teaspoon grated orange zest

2 tablespoons butter

12 slices day-old bread, cut ½ inch thick

¾ cup raisins (optional)

1. Preheat the oven to 325°F, with a rack placed in the center of the oven.

2. In a large mixing bowl, whisk together the yolks, sugar, half-and-half, rum (if using), vanilla, nutmeg, cinnamon, and orange zest until well combined.

3. Butter the slices of bread and arrange them to fit in a 9 × 13-inch baking dish. Sprinkle the raisins (if using) over the bread. Pour the custard slowly over the bread; let sit for about 10 minutes. You may have to push the bread into the custard to guarantee no bread remains dry.

4. Cover loosely with foil, poking a few holes in the top to allow steam to escape. Bake for about 1 hour, remove foil, and bake until golden brown, or until the center is just firm.

5. Remove from the oven and allow to stand for 10 minutes. Serve warm.

VARIATION: CARAMELIZED APPLE BREAD PUDDING

I large or 2 small apples, cored and cut into ¼-inch dice

2 tablespoons unsalted butter

3 tablespoons brown sugar

2 tablespoons brandy or I teaspoon lemon juice

Sauté the apples in the butter over medium heat, add the brown sugar and brandy, and cook until the apples are tender. Follow the Bread and Butter Pudding recipe, but add the caramelized apples to the mix before baking.

Chocolate-Cherry Bread Pudding

Makes 8 servings

3 cups half-and-half

¾ cup well-packed brown sugar

½ pound bittersweet chocolate, finely chopped

4 tablespoons (½ stick) unsalted butter, cut in ½-inch slices

3 large eggs plus 2 egg yolks

6 cups cubed day-old baked Chocolate Bread (page 85), Brioche (page 65), or Challah (page 147)

1½ cups pitted sour cherries

1. Preheat the oven to 325°F, with a rack placed in the center of the oven.

2. In a small saucepan, bring the half-and-half and brown sugar to a simmer. Remove from the heat and add the chocolate and butter, stirring until the chocolate is completely melted and smooth. Allow the mixture to cool slightly, about 5 minutes.

3. Whisk together the eggs and egg yolks and add to the cooled chocolate mixture.

4. Arrange the cubed bread and cherries in a 9 × 13-inch baking dish. Pour the chocolate custard over the bread and allow it to sit for 15 minutes. You may have to push the bread down into the custard to make sure it is well soaked.

5. Cover loosely with foil, poking a few holes in the top to allow steam to escape. Bake for about 50 minutes, or until the center is firm to the touch.

6. Allow to sit for 10 minutes before serving.

Almond Bostock

This is a very pastry chef–esque way to use up stale bread. It's just toast that's been sweetened with a bit of rose-scented simple syrup and baked with almond cream. It's all very easy to do, but it results in a super-decadent piece of toast. See the variation to make it even more decadent. Lyle's Golden Syrup is a sweet, amber-colored inverted cane sugar (liquid, not crystals) that looks and behaves just like honey, but has a distinct and lovely flavor.

Makes 8 slices

> 8 (½-inch-thick) slices Brioche (page 65) or any other bread you want
>
> 2 tablespoons Lyle's Golden Syrup, honey, or sugar
>
> 2 tablespoons water
>
> 2½ teaspoons grated orange zest
>
> ½ teaspoon rose water (optional)
>
> I cup Almond Cream (page 357)
>
> ½ cup sliced natural almonds (raw)
>
> ¼ cup sugar
>
> Edible dried rose petals (optional)

1. **Preheat the oven to 350°F,** with a rack placed in the center of the oven.

2. Lay the slices of bread on a baking sheet lined with parchment paper or a silicone mat.

3. Heat the golden syrup, the water, ½ teaspoon of the orange zest, and the rose water (if using) until well combined.

4. Brush the golden syrup mixture over the slices of bread.

5. Spread the almond cream evenly over the slices.

6. Mix together the sliced almonds, the sugar, the remaining 2 teaspoons orange zest, and the rose petals (if using) and sprinkle over the almond cream.

7. Bake until golden brown, about 15 minutes.

RASPBERRY VARIATION:

Follow the Almond Bostock recipe, but after brushing the bread slices with the syrup mixture, spread 1 tablespoon raspberry jam over each slice. Continue as directed.

16

FLAKY DOUGH

Since our first book came out, we've had many requests for a quicker version of croissants and Danish. Everyone loves a flaky croissant and rich, buttery Danish, but no one seems to enjoy all the work that goes into making them. These pastries are made with laminated doughs, which just means there are layers of butter sandwiched between layers of dough. The trick is to get many of these thin layers all stacked up, so when the dough hits the oven, it rises into flaky puffs of ethereal glory.

The traditional method, which this resembles, can take hours, and the conditions have to be just so. Given that our book is based on creating wonderful breads in less time, we didn't feel right asking you to devote a day to this process. We made some compromises so you can have the magic without all the labor. Our versions may not be quite as rich, because the compromise was to use less butter, but they are so wonderfully flaky and it takes only about 15 minutes to prepare the dough. Once you've done it once or twice, you'll be able to shave even more time off the process.

Danish-ish and Croissant-esque Dough

These recipes start with a dough that is made with bread flour, because the dough has more strength and stretch than those made with all-purpose flour. You really can make these with many doughs in the book, but it will just require a more delicate hand, so for your first try, use one of the doughs we list below. Danish is made with a dough enriched with eggs, so we'll use our Challah dough as the base. Croissants are made without eggs, so we'll start with our Super Strong Dough and add layers of butter.

  1 pound (grapefruit-size portion) Super Strong dough (for croissants) (page 59)
  or
  1 pound (grapefruit-size portion) Challah dough (for Danish) (page 147)
  All-purpose flour, for dusting
  12 tablespoons (1½ sticks) unsalted butter, at room temperature

1. Dust the surface of the refrigerated dough with flour and cut off a 1-pound (grapefruit-size) piece. Dust the piece with more flour and quickly shape it into a rough ball by stretching the surface of the dough around to the bottom, rotating the ball a quarter-turn as you go.

2. Using a rolling pin, roll the dough out into a ⅛-inch-thick rectangle, about 11 × 14 inches. As you roll out the dough, add flour as needed to prevent sticking. **Place the dough in the refrigerator to chill for at least 15 minutes before adding the butter.** (The dough needs to be cold, or it will be too sticky to do your folds and the butter may bust through. See sidebar on page 337.)

3. Cut the butter into ½ tablespoon–size pieces and space them evenly over two-thirds of the chilled dough, leaving about a ½-inch border around the edge.

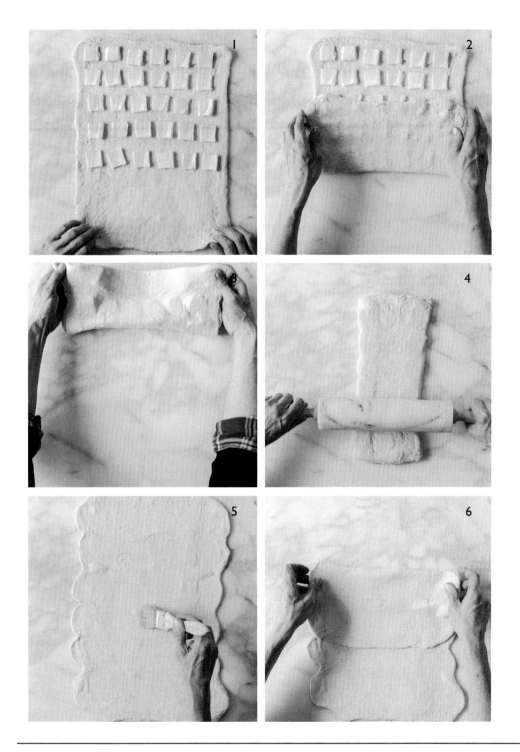

Visit BreadIn5.com, where you'll find recipes, photos, videos, and instructional material.

335

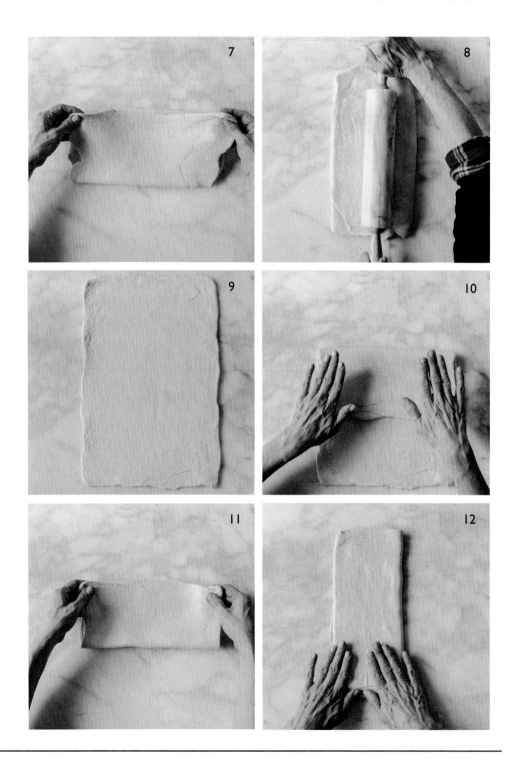

4. Fold the third of dough that doesn't have butter on it over the butter, to the center, and then fold the remaining buttered dough over the center, so it is like a letter.

5. Roll the dough out into a rectangle as close to the original size (11 × 14 inches) as possible. Start by rolling the width. If the dough fights you, just let it sit for a few minutes. If your kitchen is warm, let it sit, covered, in the refrigerator.

6. Once it is 11 × 14 inches, fold in thirds again, repeating the letter fold. Brush off any flour that you used while rolling, so the layers will stick to one another.

7. Repeat this whole process one more time and refrigerate for an hour before using (or store in the refrigerator for 5 days or freeze for up to 2 weeks).

8. You are now ready to use the dough in any of the recipes in this chapter or for several pastries throughout the book.

BUTTER TEMPERATURE MATTERS: For the dough to come together in a reasonable amount of time, with ease, it is important to have the butter at room temperature. It should still be solid, so if your kitchen is 90 degrees and the butter is wilting in the butter dish, this is not the recipe to work on. Maybe flip on the AC or wait for a cooler day. If the butter is too soft, it will just squish around and be hard to roll the layers without the butter escaping out the sides. If the butter is too cold, it may just cut through the dough.

Croissant-esque Rolls

These are so close to the real thing, but we just couldn't bring ourselves to claim you'll never notice a difference from their Parisian cousin. In traditional recipes, the weight of the butter and dough are equal, which means the croissants are buttery beyond belief and the layers fly high into the sky. These are a touch more modest, which matches our Minnesotan ways, but we find they are still fantastic; plus, they're less time-consuming and we don't miss the extra butter.

Makes 5 large croissants

I batch Croissant-esque Dough (page 334)
Egg wash (I egg beaten with I tablespoon water), for brushing the croissants

1. Line a baking sheet with parchment paper

2. Using a rolling pin, roll the dough out into a ¼-inch-thick rectangle that measures about 8 × 12 inches.

3. Cut triangles that are 8 inches long and 4 inches wide at the base. You should get about 5 large croissants from the batch; plus, you will have scraps from the 2 ends, which can be used in Cinnamon Twists and Turns (page 196).

4. Take one of the triangles and make a ¼-inch cut in the center of the short end. Stretch that end out a bit and then roll the dough until you get to the pointy end, tucking it under the dough so that it won't pop up while baking. Place on the baking sheet. Repeat with the remaining pieces of dough, cover loosely with plastic wrap, and allow to rest at room temperature for 90 minutes.

5. Preheat the oven to 425°F, with a rack placed in the center of the oven.

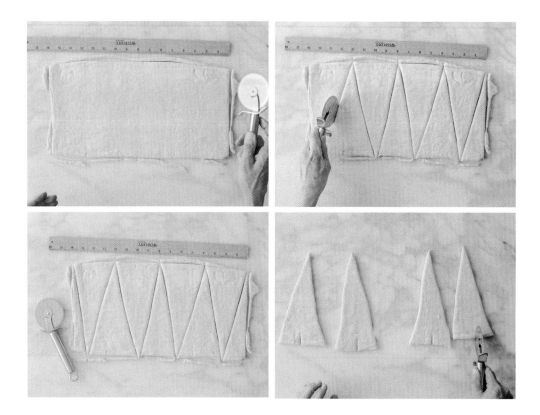

6. Brush the croissants with egg wash and bake for 30 minutes, or until deeply browned and set.

7. Allow to cool slightly before serving.

VARIATION: ALMOND CROISSANTS
Makes 5 croissants

1 batch Croissant-esque Dough
   (page 336)
1 cup Almond Cream (page 359) or
   almond paste
¼ cup confectioners' sugar

1½ tablespoons heavy cream
¼ teaspoon almond extract
¼ cup sliced almonds, toasted
Egg wash (1 egg beaten with 1 tablespoon
   water), for brushing the croissants

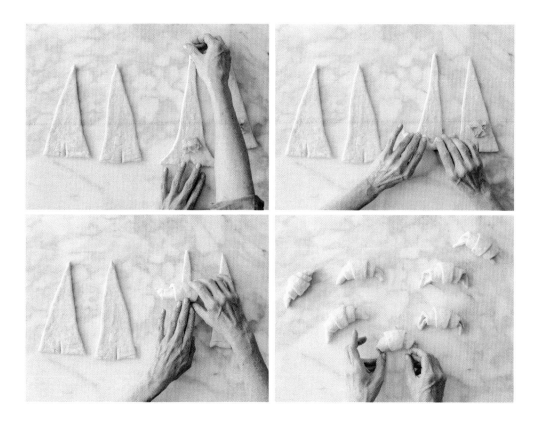

1. Line a baking sheet with parchment paper.

2. Using a rolling pin, roll the dough out into a ¼-inch-thick rectangle that measures about 8 × 12 inches.

3. Cut triangles that are 4 inches wide at the base. You should get about 5 large croissants from the batch; plus, you will have scraps from the 2 ends which can be used in Cinnamon Twists and Turns (page 196).

4. Make a ¼-inch cut in the center of the wide end of each piece of dough. Stretch that end out a bit to make it wider. Divide the filling evenly and put it just below the cut on the wide end of the dough. Roll the dough over the filling until you get to the pointy end, tucking it under the dough so that it won't pop up while baking. Place them on the baking sheet, spaced so they won't touch. Cover loosely with plastic wrap and allow to rest at room temperature for 90 minutes.

5. Preheat the oven to 400°F, with a rack placed in the bottom third of the oven.

6. Brush the croissants with egg wash and bake for 30 minutes, or until deeply browned and set.

7. Allow to cool.

8. To make icing: Mix the confectioners' sugar, cream, and almond extract in a small bowl. Drizzle over cooled croissants. Top with toasted almonds.

VARIATION: CHOCOLATE CROISSANTS
Makes 8 croissants

1 batch Croissant-esque Dough (page 334)

4 ounces chocolate (use a thin bar, so you can have clean pieces and not chips), cut into 8 pieces

Egg wash (1 egg beaten with 1 tablespoon water), for brushing the croissants

4 ounces chocolate, melted

1. Line 2 baking sheets with parchment paper.

2. Using a rolling pin, roll the dough out into a ¼-inch-thick rectangle, about 12 × 12 inches.

3. Cut the dough into four 3-inch strips and then cut the strips in half crosswise, so you end up with 8 rectangles that are 3 × 6 inches.

4. Place a piece of chocolate at one end of a dough rectangle and roll up the dough, concealing the chocolate. Make sure the end is tucked under the dough, so that it

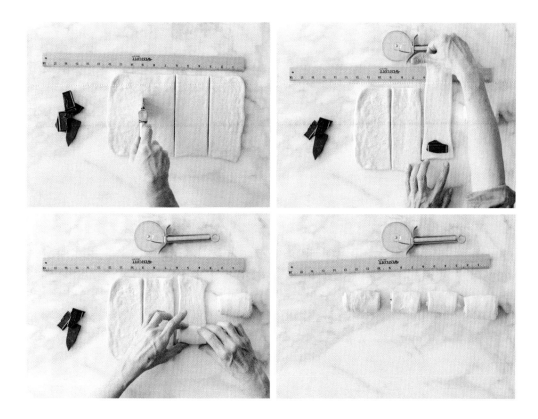

won't pop up while baking. Place on a baking sheet. Repeat with the remaining pieces of dough. Cover loosely with plastic wrap and allow to rest at room temperature for 90 minutes.

5. Preheat the oven to 425°F, with a rack placed in the center of the oven.

6. Brush the croissants with egg wash and bake for 30 minutes, or until deeply browned and set.

7. Allow to cool slightly, then drizzle with melted chocolate. The chocolate will be gooey if they're still warm, but still excellent even after it has solidified.

Turnovers

These are little packages of flaky dough encasing just about any filling you can imagine. We've made some sweet suggestions in the recipe, but as long as you stick to our amounts, you can play with your own combinations, including savory (ham and cheese would be fun).

Makes 12 pastries

I batch Danish-ish or Croissant-esque Dough (page 334)

All-purpose flour, for dusting

2 cups sugar, for rolling (flour if you're going savory)

I cup Cream Cheese Filling (page 313), Pastry Cream (page 354), Farmer Cheese Filling (page 362), and/or Applesauce (page 358)

I cup Quick Jam (page 351), Poppy Seed Filling (page 361), or Prune or Apricot Filling (page 360)

1. Line 2 baking sheets with parchment paper.

2. Using a rolling pin, roll the dough out into a ⅛-inch-thick rectangle, about 12 × 16 inches, adding flour as needed to prevent sticking.

3. Cut out twelve 4-inch squares using a pastry or pizza cutter.

4. Cover a work surface with a generous coating of the sugar. Lay one of the squares in the sugar. Using a rolling pin, roll back and forth over 2 of the points opposite each other, until they are about 1/16 inch thick. If the dough sticks to the rolling pin, dust the pin with a bit of flour. Lay the dough on a lined baking sheet. Repeat with the rest of the dough squares, placing 6 on a sheet and keeping them at least 1 inch apart.

5. Spread 2 tablespoons of the cream cheese filling in the center of each sugared dough square. Spoon 2 tablespoons of jam over the cream cheese. Brush egg wash over one of the rolled points and fold the other rolled point over the filling, pressing it down to seal the point over the filling. Fold the egg-washed point over and try to tuck it under the bottom to prevent it from popping up during baking. Cover loosely with plastic wrap and allow to rest at room temperature for 45 minutes.

6. Preheat the oven to 400°F, with a rack placed in the center of the oven.

7. Dust with more sugar and bake for about 20 minutes, or until the dough is golden brown and the sugar is nicely caramelized.

8. Serve warm or cooled.

Queen, Oh Man! (Kouign Amann)

These caramelized muffin-shaped croissants are fit for a queen or just an afternoon snack. They are made with butter-layered dough and rolled in sugar, so when they hit the oven they puff up and have a sugary crust on the outside.

Makes 12 pastries

I batch Croissant-esque Dough (page 334)
Butter, for the muffin pan
2 cups sugar
Pinch sea salt

1. Generously grease 12 muffin cups with butter and sprinkle with sugar.

2. Sprinkle a work surface with a thick layer of sugar, lay down the dough, and sprinkle more sugar on top. Using a rolling pin, roll the dough out into a ⅛-inch-thick rectangle, about 12 × 16 inches, adding more sugar as you go to prevent it from sticking to the surface and forming a thick crust of sugar.

3. Cut out twelve 4-inch squares using a pastry or pizza cutter.

4. Collect the 4 corners of 1 dough square together and slip the dough into the prepared muffin cup. Repeat with the rest of the dough. Cover loosely with plastic wrap and allow to rest at room temperature for 45 minutes.

5. Preheat the oven to 400°F, with a rack placed in the center of the oven.

6. Dust with more sugar and bake for about 20 minutes, or until the dough is golden brown and the sugar is nicely caramelized.

7. Serve warm or cooled.

VARIATION: FRUIT FILLED

1. Grease 8 muffin cups with butter and sprinkle with sugar.

2. Sprinkle a work surface with a thick layer of sugar, lay down the dough, and sprinkle more sugar on top. Using a rolling pin, roll the dough out into a ⅛-inch thick rectangle, about 12 × 16 inches, adding more sugar as you go, to prevent it from sticking to the surface and forming a thick crust of sugar.

3. Cut 8 squares, using a pastry or pizza cutter.

4. Lay the dough into the prepared muffin cups, the dough will hang over the edge slightly. Add 2 tablespoons of applesauce (page 358) or any of the Quick Jams (page 351) to the center of each cup. Cover loosely with plastic wrap and allow to rest at room temperature for 45 minutes.

5. Preheat the oven to 400°F, with a rack placed in the center of the oven.

6. Dust with more sugar and bake for about 20 minutes, or until the dough is golden brown and the sugar is nicely caramelized.

7. Serve warm or cooled.

17

QUICK JAMS AND FILLINGS

Quick Raspberry Jam

This is a super-fast way to make homemade jam with a wonderful flavor and texture and vibrant color. Because it is only relying on the natural pectin in the fruit, it will be a tiny bit looser than jam you buy in the store, but if you cook it as long as we say, it will have lots of body. This is not a true canning technique, so only plan to have this around for a few weeks, stored in the refrigerator.

Makes about 1 cup jam

  1 pound fresh or frozen raspberries
  ½ cup sugar
  1 tablespoon lemon juice

Place the raspberries, sugar, and lemon juice in a saucepan and use a fork to break up the raspberries just enough to produce a bit of juice. Simmer over medium-low heat for

about 30 minutes, stirring often. The jam is ready when it clings to the spoon and you can draw a line through the jam that doesn't immediately fill in. Allow to cool before using.

VARIATIONS: OTHER QUICK FRUIT JAMS

This method works for just about any fruit. You'll want to adjust the sugar or use honey, depending on your taste and the sweetness of the fruit you pick. The amount of time it takes to reduce the liquids in the fruits will depend on the fruit, so it may take longer or shorter to make.

Blueberries
Cherries
Concord grapes (use more sugar; they're pretty tart)
Peaches (blanch and peel them first) or other stone fruits
Strawberries

Pastry Cream

Pastry cream is a staple in the pastry kitchen. To flavor this silky custard, you can use pure vanilla extract or try a vanilla bean, which gives the most intense and satisfying flavor. If you have never tried baking with a real vanilla bean, try it now and you'll be hooked. To use the bean, just slice it lengthwise with a paring knife to expose the seeds. Scrape the seeds out of the pod and throw the seeds and the pod into your saucepan. The pod will get strained out at the end, leaving the fragrant aroma and the flecks of real vanilla behind.

Makes 3 cups pastry cream

2 cups milk

½ cup sugar

2 tablespoons unsalted butter

Pinch salt

½ vanilla bean or 1 teaspoon pure vanilla extract

2 tablespoons cornstarch

1 large egg plus 3 egg yolks

1. Bring the milk, ¼ cup of the sugar, the butter, the salt, and the vanilla bean to a gentle boil in a medium-to-large saucepan. Remove from the heat.

2. Whisk together the cornstarch and the remaining ¼ cup sugar. Add the egg and egg yolks to the cornstarch, and mix into a smooth paste.

3. Slowly, and in small amounts, whisk a little of the hot milk into the egg mixture. Once the egg mixture is warm to the touch, pour it back into the milk in the pan.

4. Return the custard to the stove and bring to a boil, whisking continuously, for 2 to 3 minutes, or until thickened.

5. Strain the pastry cream into a shallow container and cover with plastic wrap pressed directly on the surface to keep a skin from forming.

6. Set the container in the freezer for 15 minutes, and then refrigerate.

VARIATION: MAPLE PASTRY CREAM
Add 3 tablespoons maple syrup to the finished custard.

Lemon Curd

Makes 2 cups lemon curd

6 egg yolks

I cup sugar

½ cup lemon juice

I tablespoon grated lemon zest

8 tablespoons (I stick) unsalted butter, cut into I-tablespoon pieces

1. Whisk together the yolks, sugar, lemon juice, and lemon zest in a large metal bowl.

2. Place the bowl over a pot of gently simmering water set up as a double boiler.

3. Stir constantly with a rubber spatula until the lemon curd begins to thicken, about 10 minutes.

4. Add the butter and continue to stir until it is completely melted and the curd is quite thick; it will be the consistency of smooth pudding.

5. If there are any lumps, strain the curd into a container; then, cover with plastic wrap.

6. Set the container in the freezer until cool, and then refrigerate.

Almond Cream

"I'd never had homemade almond cream before I met Zoë and we started writing cookbooks together. It's standard fare for pastry chefs, but wildly impressive when home cooks whip it up. It's incredibly easy to prepare, but the flavor is a revelation. In some of the sweet recipes, we give you a choice for a creamy filling, but I always choose this one if I have a minute to mix a few ingredients—it beautifully complements just about any tart fruit." —Jeff

Makes 1 cup

4 tablespoons (½ stick) unsalted butter, at room temperature

½ cup almond paste

¼ cup all-purpose flour

1 large egg

¼ teaspoon orange flower water (optional)

¼ teaspoon almond extract

Process the butter, almond paste, flour, egg, orange flower water (if using), and almond extract in a food processor until smooth and well combined.

Applesauce

Homemade applesauce could not be easier and beats anything you can buy in a jar. We leave the skins on for ease and for the beautiful color. The flavor and texture are just incredible for recipes like Kolache (page 309) and Turnovers (page 345) we really recommend you make it yourself. Having said that, of course you can buy really high-quality applesauce in the store and it will save you some time.

Makes 2 cups applesauce

4 apples, peeled or skins on, cored and diced

¼ cup honey (adjust for desired sweetness)

½ teaspoon ground cinnamon

1 teaspoon lemon juice

Pinch salt

Cook the apples, honey, cinnamon, and salt over medium-low heat until the fruit is tender. Some of the fruit will break down into a sauce, while other pieces may stay whole. This will somewhat depend on how long you cook it. You can leave the applesauce chunky or blend it smooth—we'll leave that to your personal preference; it doesn't matter for the recipes.

APPLES: "When I was growing up, there were two varieties of apples that I was aware of: Red Delicious and McIntosh. One was pretty, but despite its name, it tasted like chalk; the other was little and not so pretty, but tasty. Today, there are dozens to apples to choose from at the supermarket. The University of Minnesota, which is just down the street, has developed thirty varieties. I like to use more than one type of apple when baking, because they have such different flavor profiles (sweet to tart) and textures (firm to saucy). Try to pick apples that cross all of these profiles and you'll end up with the most interesting cake. They will vary depending on the season and where you live, but here are some of my favorites:" —Zoë

- Fireside/Connell Red is sweet and will break down slightly when cooked.
- Haralson is tart and will hold its shape when baked.
- Prairie Spy has a balance of sweet and tart and will stay firm when cooked.
- Honey Gold is a sweet apple that is really juicy but holds its shape well when cooked.

Prune or Apricot Fillings

Many breads and pastries are filled with cooked compotes of dried fruits that are rich and flavorful.

Makes about 1 cup filling

PRUNE

2 cups (10 ounces) pitted prunes

1½ cups water

½ orange, supremed and cut into ½-inch
   dice (see sidebar, page 361)

½ teaspoon ground cinnamon

⅛ teaspoon ground cloves

1 tablespoon honey

APRICOT

2 cups dried apricots, chopped into
   ¼-inch dice

1 cup orange juice

½ cup honey

1 teaspoon grated lemon zest

2 tablespoons rum (optional)

To make the prune or the apricot filling, place the ingredients in a medium saucepan and simmer until the fruit is soft and the mixture is very thick. (If it is too runny, it won't stay put when baked on the dough.) Cool to room temperature, then refrigerate. Can be made several days ahead.

SUPREME: Supreming is a way of removing the hard, bitter rind and stringy membranes from the orange, so you are just left with the soft fruit within. To do so, use a sharp knife to trim the top and bottom rind, so it will sit flat, and then cut off the outer rind and pith down to the orange flesh within. Once all the outer pith is removed, cut the sections of orange away from the membrane. Do this by slicing into the center of the orange as close to the membrane as possible; the section will just fall away once you do both sides.

Poppy Seed Filling

Makes about 2 cups filling

2 cups poppy seeds, ground in a coffee grinder (some will be pulverized and some will stay intact, which is fine)

1 cup milk

1 cup sugar

2 tablespoons lemon juice

2 teaspoons grated lemon zest

1 teaspoon ground cinnamon

Place the ingredients in a saucepan and simmer over low heat until the mixture is very thick. (If it is too runny, it won't stay put when baked on the dough.) Can be used right away or stored in the refrigerator for up to 2 weeks.

Farmer Cheese Filling

Farmer cheese is like a cross between cottage cheese and cream cheese. It has a delicate flavor and wonderful texture. You can often find it in the dairy case of your grocer.

Makes about 2 cups filling

    4 ounces cream cheese

    ¼ cup sugar

    1 teaspoon vanilla extract

    2 tablespoons matzo cake meal or all-purpose flour

    1 pound soft farmer cheese

    1 large egg

Mix the cream cheese, sugar, vanilla, and matzo meal until smooth. Add the farmer cheese and egg, and mix to combine.

SOURCES

FOR BREAD-BAKING PRODUCTS:

Bob's Red Mill: BobsRedMill.com, 800-349-2173

Emile Henry cookware: EmileHenryUSA.com, 302-326-4800

Mauviel: MauvielUSA.com, 302-326-4803

Gold Medal Flour: GoldMedalFlour.com, 800-248-7310

King Arthur Flour: KingArthurFlour.com/shop, 800-827-6836

Nordic Ware: Nordicware.com, 877-466-7342

Penzeys Spices: Penzeys.com, 800-741-7787

Red Star Yeast: RedStarYeast.com, 800-445-4746

CONSULTED:

United States Department of Agriculture Fact Sheet. *Egg Products Preparation: Shell Eggs from Farm to Table.* http://www.fsis.usda.gov/wps/portal/fsis/topics/food-safety-education/get-answers/food-safety-fact-sheets/egg-products-preparation/shell-eggs-from-farm-to-table/CT_Index, accessed September 23, 2012.

INDEX